Social Studies Skills Made Easy

BY
MYRL SHIREMAN

COPYRIGHT © 1999 Mark Twain Media, Inc.

ISBN 1–58037–097–7

Printing No. CD-1330

Mark Twain Media, Inc., Publishers
Distributed by Carson-Dellosa Publishing Company, Inc.

Table of Contents

Introduction iv

United States Geography 1
    Map I 3
    United States Crossword Puzzle 4
    Physical Features in the United States 5
    U.S. Physical Features Crossword Puzzle 6
    Rivers in the United States 7
    Capital Cities 8
    Head for the Border 9
    Regions of the United States 10
        Map II: The Northeast 10
        Map III: The Midwest 11
        Map IV: The Southeast 11
        Map V: The West 12
    Name That State: Part I 13
    Name That State: Part II 15
    Name That State: Part III 17
    Name That State: Part IV 19
    Name That State: Part V 21
    Name That State: Part VI 23
    Name That State: Part VII 24
    Reading and Using Road Maps: Part I 26
    Reading and Using Road Maps: Part II 27

Maps and Graphs 28
    Map Measurements 28
    Size of the United States Compared to Other Nations 29
    Using Graphs to Show Information: Circle Graphs 30
    Learning About Population Pyramids 32
    Line and Bar Graphs and Population Trends 33
    Population Density 37
    Elevation and Contour Maps 39
    More Elevation Practice 42
    Understanding Temperature Maps 43

Table of Contents (continued)

The Government of the United States **45**

    Legislative Branch 45

        The House of Representatives 45

        House of Representatives Review 47

        The Senate 48

        Legislation 49

    The Executive Branch 50

    Branches of the U.S. Government Crossword Puzzle 52

    Electing the President and Vice President 53

        The Electoral College and the Popular Vote 53

    U.S. Presidents 59

    Presidential Time Line 62

The U.S. Economic System **65**

    Understanding Capitalism 65

        Capitalism Crossword Puzzle 68

        Ownership of Business 69

    Learning About the Stock Market 71

        Stock Growth, Dividends, and Yield 73

        Reading Quotes From the Stock Market 75

        Stock Market Crossword Puzzle 76

    Learning About Supply and Demand 77

        Great Taste Candies 78

    Learning About Social Security 82

    How Far Will the Money Go? 84

Answer Keys **85**

Introduction

This activity book is written to serve as a supplement to reinforce social science teaching in the middle school. Historically, middle school social studies texts have emphasized the historical perspective. Undoubtedly, the historical perspective is of utmost importance in understanding the United States.

The material in this activity book is designed to help students see the relationships among history, geography, government, and economics in the United States. All of these aspects of social studies must be seen together to help middle school students develop a better understanding of the nation's past, present, and future.

In today's middle school classrooms, teachers are striving to ensure that middle school students possess the social studies background required to pursue an increasingly rigorous secondary social studies program. Secondary students cannot perform the required higher-level thinking without a solid background in all aspects of social science. This book is designed to prepare middle school students for the challenges they will face in secondary school.

Name _____ Date _____

United States Geography

Refer to a copy of Map I and complete the following exercise.

1. Locate each state on Map I by placing the two-letter abbreviation for each state within the boundary of each state. For example, Arkansas = AR and Illinois = IL.

2. Place a dot and the name of the city on Map I to locate each of the following cities.

Springfield, IL	**Los Angeles**	**San Francisco**	**Portland**
Seattle	**Phoenix**	**Tucson**	**Reno**
Las Vegas	**Billings**	**Salt Lake City**	**Provo**
Boise	**Pocatello**	**Denver**	**Colorado Springs**
Albuquerque	**Santa Fe**	**Sioux Falls**	**Bismarck**
Fargo	**Wichita**	**Oklahoma City**	**Fort Worth**
Dallas	**Houston**	**Minneapolis**	**St. Paul**
Omaha	**Des Moines**	**Kansas City**	**St. Louis**
Chicago	**Little Rock**	**Baton Rouge**	**New Orleans**
Milwaukee	**Indianapolis**	**Louisville**	**Birmingham**
Mobile	**Jackson**	**Natchez**	**Atlanta**
Jacksonville, FL	**Tampa**	**Miami**	**Savannah**
Raleigh	**Charlotte**	**Charleston**	**Pittsburgh**
Philadelphia	**Norfolk**	**New York City**	**Boston**
Columbus	**Cincinnati**	**Buffalo**	**Bangor**
Concord	**Hartford**	**Montpelier**	**Washington, D.C.**

3. Match the capital city in Column B with the corresponding state in Column A.

Column A	**Column B**
_____ a. Texas	1. Springfield
_____ b. Tennessee	2. Juneau
_____ c. Oregon	3. Albany
_____ d. Hawaii	4. Austin
_____ e. Alaska	5. Jackson
_____ f. New York	6. Tallahassee
_____ g. Florida	7. Little Rock
_____ h. Illinois	8. Salem
_____ i. Mississippi	9. Nashville
_____ j. Arkansas	10. Honolulu

Name_____ Date _____

4. The following cities have the largest populations. Look up each city in an almanac or encyclopedia and place the cities in order from the smallest to the largest on the blanks below. Also, fill in the population and state for each city. Then locate and label the cities on a fresh copy of Map I.

| Houston | New York | Los Angeles | Chicago | Philadelphia |
| Detroit | Dallas | Atlanta | Boston | Washington, D.C. |

City	Population	State
a.		
b.		
c.		
d.		
e.		
f.		
g.		
h.		
i.		
j.		

5. There are some states in the United States that do not have a border on a river, gulf, lake, or ocean. Check a U.S. map or an atlas and circle the states below that do not have a major part of their boundaries on a river, gulf, lake, or ocean.

Utah	Idaho	Kansas	California	Arizona
Oklahoma	Minnesota	Texas	Montana	New Mexico
Massachusetts				

6. Refer to the above list of states and a U.S. map or atlas. Write the names of the states that do have a boundary on a river, gulf, lake, or ocean. Write the name of the river, gulf, lake, or ocean that the state borders. (A state may have more than one water border.)

State	River	Gulf	Lake	Ocean
a.				
b.				
c.				
d.				
e.				
f.				
g.				
h.				

Name _____ Date _____

Map I: The United States

Name_____ Date_____

United States Crossword Puzzle

Use the clues below to complete the crossword puzzle about states. You may need to refer to an encyclopedia, atlas, or other resource to find the answers.

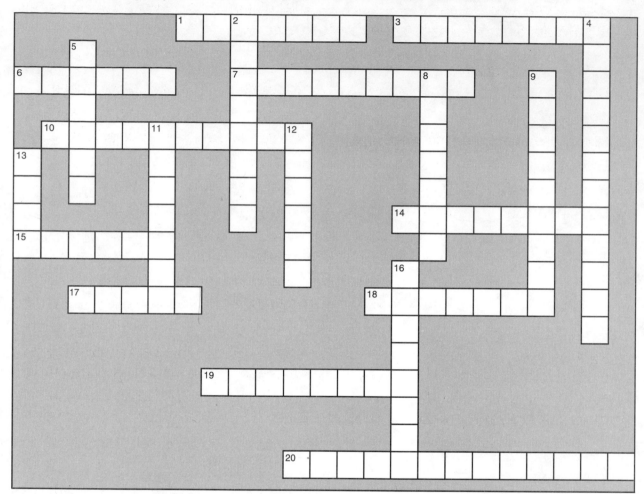

ACROSS

1. This southwestern state contains the Grand Canyon.
3. The largest city of this state is near Windsor, Canada.
6. This northwestern state contains Crater Lake National Park.
7. This state has a city that is a large port at the mouth of the Mississippi River.
10. This state was the site of the Gold Rush of 1849.
14. The capital of this state is Little Rock.
15. This state is a group of islands.
17. The capital of this state is Austin.
18. The "peach" state is located in the southeastern United States.
19. This state was once known as Indian Territory.
20. This New England state was settled by Pilgrims and Puritans.

DOWN

2. The largest city in this state is located in the northeast corner of the state on Lake Michigan.
4. This northeastern state contains the White Mountains (two words).
5. The capital of this state is Carson City.
8. The capital of this state is Albany (two words).
9. The capital of this state is St. Paul.
11. This state is a peninsula.
12. Part of this state is north of the Arctic Circle.
13. The capital of this state is Salt Lake City.
16. The capital of this state has the same name as a famous U.S. president whose term was during the Civil War.

Name_____ Date _____

Physical Features in the United States

Using a U.S. map or an atlas and a blank copy of Map I, place the following physical features on the map. Place the symbol (if there is one) on the map and write the name to identify the physical feature on the map. Next to each physical feature listed below are state names. Circle the state or states where the feature is located.

Physical Feature	Symbol	State(s)
1. Rocky Mountains	/R\	Colorado/Montana/Missouri/Alabama
2. Appalachian Mountains	/A\	Colorado/Nevada/Virginia/Tennessee
3. Sierra Nevada Mountains	/S\	California/Texas/Mississippi/Iowa
4. Great Basin		Tennessee/Idaho/Nevada/Florida
5. Sonoran Desert	(cactus)	Montana/Alaska/California
6. Ozark Plateau		Illinois/Arkansas/Missouri/Ohio
7. Lake Okeechobee		New Mexico/Texas/Florida/Iowa
8. Great Salt Lake		Utah/New York/Kansas/Oregon
9. Lake Superior		Minnesota/Illinois/Wisconsin/Texas
10. Lake Michigan		Minnesota/Michigan/Illinois/Indiana
11. Lake Erie		Ohio/New York/Kentucky/Maine
12. Lake Ontario		Tennessee/New York/Pennsylvania
13. Lake Huron		Michigan/Arkansas/Idaho/Georgia
14. Mississippi River	~~~	Arkansas/Mississippi/Missouri/Iowa
15. Ohio River	~~~	Illinois/Ohio/Indiana/Kentucky
16. Missouri River	~~~	Texas/Nebraska/Iowa/South Dakota
17. Rio Grande River	~~~	Texas/New Mexico/Arizona/Wyoming
18. Hudson River	~~~	Alabama/Florida/New York/Vermont
19. Colorado River	~~~	Colorado/Utah/Arizona/California
20. Columbia River	~~~	Washington/Idaho/Oregon/California
21. Kentucky Lake		Tennessee/Florida/Georgia/Kentucky
22. Chesapeake Bay		North Carolina/Virginia/Maryland
23. Gulf of Mexico		Texas/Mississippi/Alabama/Florida
24. San Francisco Bay		Nevada/Texas/California/Indiana
25. Lake Champlain		New York/Vermont/Maine/Virginia
26. Lake Pontchartrain		Alabama/Virginia/Louisiana/Ohio
27. Aleutian Islands		Hawaii/Alaska/West Virginia/Iowa
28. Mount Rainier	/R\	Alaska/Colorado/Washington/Vermont
29. Mount Kea	/K\	Kansas/Idaho/Hawaii/Alaska
30. Pike's Peak	/P\	Montana/Wyoming/Utah/Colorado

Name _____ Date _____

U.S. Physical Features Crossword Puzzle

Use the clues below to complete the crossword puzzle about physical features found in the United States. You may need to refer to an encyclopedia, atlas, or other resource.

ACROSS

1. Mountains in Arkansas and Oklahoma
8. Volcanic mountain in Washington
9. Volcanic mountain in Alaska
14. Desert in California
15. Islands off the coast of Alaska
16. Largest Hawaiian island
18. Lake in Utah (three words)
19. Alaskan river

DOWN

2. Mountains in Washington and Oregon
3. Mountains that run north and south in the eastern United States
4. Northernmost point in Alaska (two words)
5. River between Missouri and Illinois
6. Sea in California
7. River that begins in Montana and ends near St. Louis
8. River between Texas and Mexico (two words)
10. Volcanic mountain in California
11. Lake between New York and Vermont (two words)
12. Lake between Wisconsin and Michigan (two words)
13. Lake in Florida
17. The Great Basin is in this state.

Name_____ Date _____

Rivers in the United States

Rivers are very important to the development of a nation. In the case of the United States, the rivers were very important in the early exploration of the interior of the continent. Settlers followed the Ohio River as the nation was settled from the east. French and Spanish explorers came up the Mississippi as they explored this new continent.

The Mississippi River drains the interior of the nation into the Gulf of Mexico. Today this large river and its tributaries are very important avenues of transportation for agricultural and other products from the interior of the nation to the Gulf of Mexico, where shipments to all parts of the world can be made.

Refer to Map I and complete the following.

1. Use a blue line and trace the path of the following rivers.

Mississippi	**Ohio**	**Tennessee**	**Allegheny**
Monongahela	**Missouri**	**Illinois**	**Arkansas**

2. Place a dot with the letter by it on the map to locate each of the following cities.

a. Pittsburgh	b. Cincinnati	c. Louisville	d. Evansville, IN
e. Paducah	f. Memphis	g. Natchez	h. Baton Rouge
i. New Orleans	j. Minneapolis	k. Davenport	l. St. Louis
m. Sioux Falls	n. Omaha	o. Kansas City	p. Chattanooga
q. Little Rock			

3. Use a blue line and trace the path of the following rivers.

Columbia	**Snake**	**Colorado**

4. In the space below, explain why the Columbia, Snake, and Colorado drain west toward the Pacific while the Missouri and Arkansas drain east to the Mississippi River.

_____

_____

_____

_____

_____

_____

7

Name _____ Date _____

Capital Cities

Write the name of the capital city on the blank beside the correct state.

Lincoln	**Helena**	**Carson City**	**Frankfort**	**Baton Rouge**
Richmond	**Olympia**	**Charleston**	**Cheyenne**	**Providence**
Topeka	**Sacramento**	**Lansing**	**Springfield**	**Boise**
Columbia	**Montgomery**	**Santa Fe**	**Des Moines**	**Pierre**
Phoenix	**Jefferson City**	**Atlanta**	**Montpelier**	**Augusta**

State   **Capital**

1. Iowa _____

2. New Mexico _____

3. Maine _____

4. California _____

5. South Carolina _____

6. New Hampshire _____

7. South Dakota _____

8. Michigan _____

9. Missouri _____

10. Kansas _____

11. Arizona _____

12. Idaho _____

13. Georgia _____

14. Alabama _____

15. Vermont _____

16. Nebraska _____

17. Washington _____

18. Virginia _____

19. Rhode Island _____

20. Kentucky _____

21. Wyoming _____

22. Nevada _____

23. Louisiana _____

24. Montana _____

25. West Virginia _____

Name_____ Date _____

Head for the Border

Refer to a map of the United States in an atlas or textbook and complete the following activity.

1. Locate the states that border the Gulf of Mexico. List the states on the blanks that follow.

_____

_____

2. Locate the states that border the Atlantic Ocean. List the states on the blanks that follow.

_____

_____

3. Locate the states that border the Pacific Ocean. List the states on the blanks that follow.

_____

_____

4. Locate the states that border Mexico. List the states on the blanks that follow.

_____

_____

5. Locate the states that border Canada. List the states on the blanks that follow.

_____

_____

Name_____ Date _____

Regions of the United States

Maps II, III, IV, and V represent major geographic regions of the United States. In national elections, the people living in these geographic regions are sometimes thought to represent a common political position on issues that are being debated. Write the names of the states found in each geographical region on the blanks below.

1. Northeast: _____

_____

_____

2. Midwest: _____

_____

_____

3. Southeast: _____

_____

_____

_____

4. West: _____

_____

_____

_____

_____

Map II: The Northeast

Name_____ Date_____

Map III: The Midwest

Map IV: The Southeast

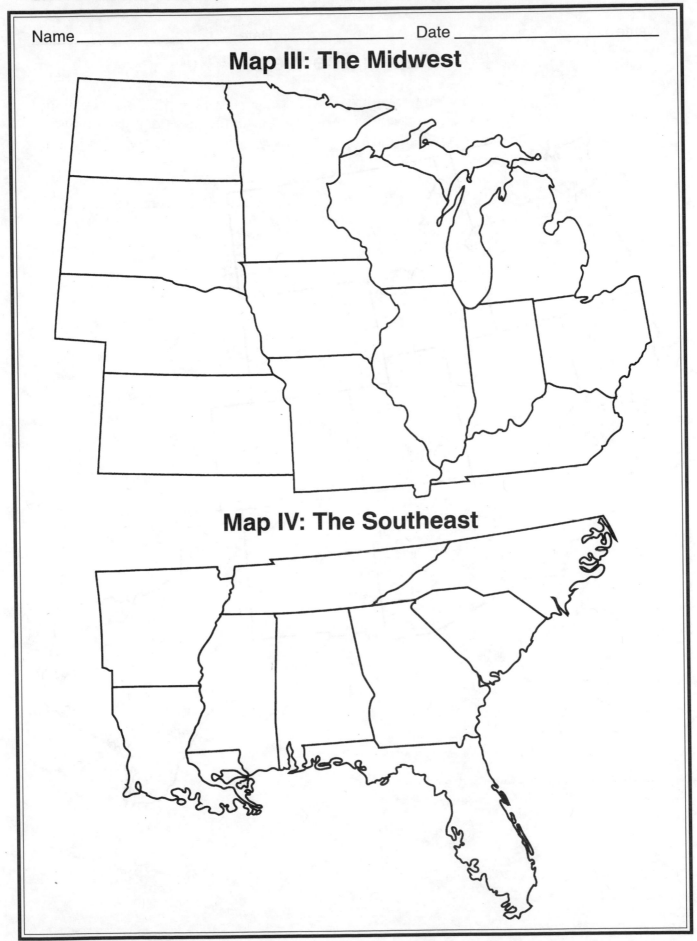

11

Name_____ Date _____

Map V: The West

Name_____ Date _____

Name That State: Part I

Each of the following paragraphs contains information that identifies one of the states listed in bold. Read each statement and write the name of the state on the blank. There may also be other information you are asked to fill in about the state. Write the answers on the blanks provided.

Tennessee   Virginia   Kentucky   West Virginia   Ohio

1. _____ The name of this state is an Indian word that means "meadow land" or "land of tomorrow." Sometimes known as the "Bluegrass State," this state is also famous for horse racing. Daniel Boone was an early explorer of this state. The northern border of this state is the Ohio River. The western boundary is the Mississippi River. The capital is a)_____ .

2. _____ The name of this state is an Iroquois word meaning "good river." Presidents Grant, Garfield, Hayes, Taft, and Harding were born in this state. Important lake ports are located on Lake Erie. Equally important river ports are located on the Ohio River, which forms the southern boundary of the state. Citizens of this state are very proud of astronauts Armstrong and Glenn, who claim this as their home state. The professional football Hall of Fame is located at Canton. The city of Akron is known as the rubber capital of the world.

3. _____ Located in this state is Mt. Vernon, the home of George Washington, and Monticello, the home of Thomas Jefferson. The Potomac River forms a boundary with Maryland. Civil War battles including Bull Run, Chancellorsville, and Fredericksburg were fought in this state. One of the original 13 colonies, this state was admitted to the Union in June of 1788. The capital city is a) _____. U.S. presidents from this state include b) _____ , c)_____ , d)_____ , e) _____ , and f) _____ .

4. _____ This state is nicknamed "The Volunteer State." The Great Smoky Mountain National Park is located in this state. The name most likely comes from "Tanasi," a name given to Cherokee villages located in parts of the state. Shiloh is the location of one of the famous battles of the Civil War, where 25,000 soldiers lost their lives. A famous river with the same name as the state flows through the state and empties into the Ohio River at Paducah, Kentucky. The Mississippi River forms the western boundary. The capital city is a) _____ . U.S. presidents elected from this state include b)_____ , c) _____, and d) _____ .

5. _____ This state, nicknamed "The Mountain State," is dominated by the Appalachian Mountains. The Monongahela River is located in the state and flows north to enter the Ohio River at Pittsburgh, Pennsylvania. The headwaters of the Potomac River begin in the Appalachians and flow north to form the border with Maryland. The capital city is Charleston.

Name_____ Date _____

6. Refer to the state maps below and locate the following: Tennessee, Virginia, Kentucky, Ohio, and West Virginia.

7. Place the name of each of the following capital cities by the dot on the map that locates the city.

Columbus   Nashville   Richmond   Charleston   Frankfort

8. Place the name of the city by the dot on the map that locates each of the following cities.

Cincinnati	**Norfolk**	**Memphis**	**Louisville**
Williamsburg	**Chattanooga**	**Morgantown**	**Youngstown**
Wheeling	**Cleveland**	**Paducah**	**Lynchburg**

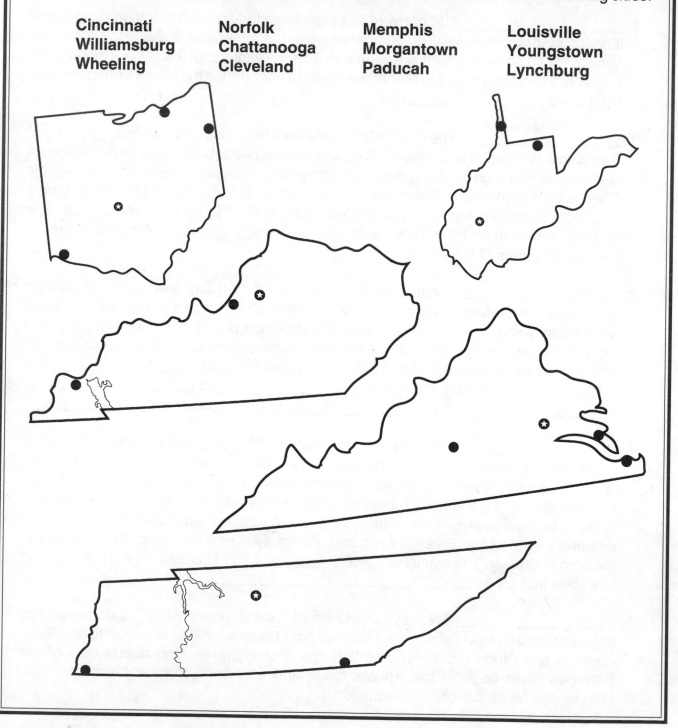

Name_____ Date _____

Name That State: Part II

Each of the following paragraphs contains information that identifies one of the states listed in bold. Read each statement and write the name of the state on the blank. There may also be other information you are asked to fill in about the state. Write the answers on the blanks provided.

Vermont   **Maine**   **New Hampshire**

1. _____ An important physical feature in this state is Mt. Washington, the highest point in the Appalachians. In this state, the Appalachians are known as the White Mountains. The White Mountains include the famous Presidential Range with peaks named for U.S. presidents. Another physical feature is the Connecticut River, which forms the western boundary with Vermont. This state is known as "The Granite State." The capital is a)_____.

2. _____ A famous lake is located in the northwest corner of this state. An important river forms the state's eastern boundary with New Hampshire. The neighbor to the west is New York. The river that forms the eastern boundary is a)_____. The famous lake in the northwest corner is b)_____. The nation located along the northern border of this state is c) _____.

3. _____ The Kennebec is the most important river in this state. The capital is Augusta. This state is bordered on the north by two provinces of Canada. Potatoes are an important agricultural crop. Lobster fishing is an important occupation for many people. The eastern boundary of the state is the a)_____ Ocean. The Canadian provinces that border this state are b) _____ and c)_____.

4. Refer to the state maps on page 16 and locate Vermont, Maine, and New Hampshire.

5. Place the name of each of the following capital cities by the dot on the map that locates the city.

   Augusta   **Montpelier**   **Concord**

6. Place the name of the city by the dot on the map that locates each of the following cities.

   Berlin   Bennington   Lewiston   Bangor
   Burlington   Nashua   Portland   Manchester

Name_____ Date _____

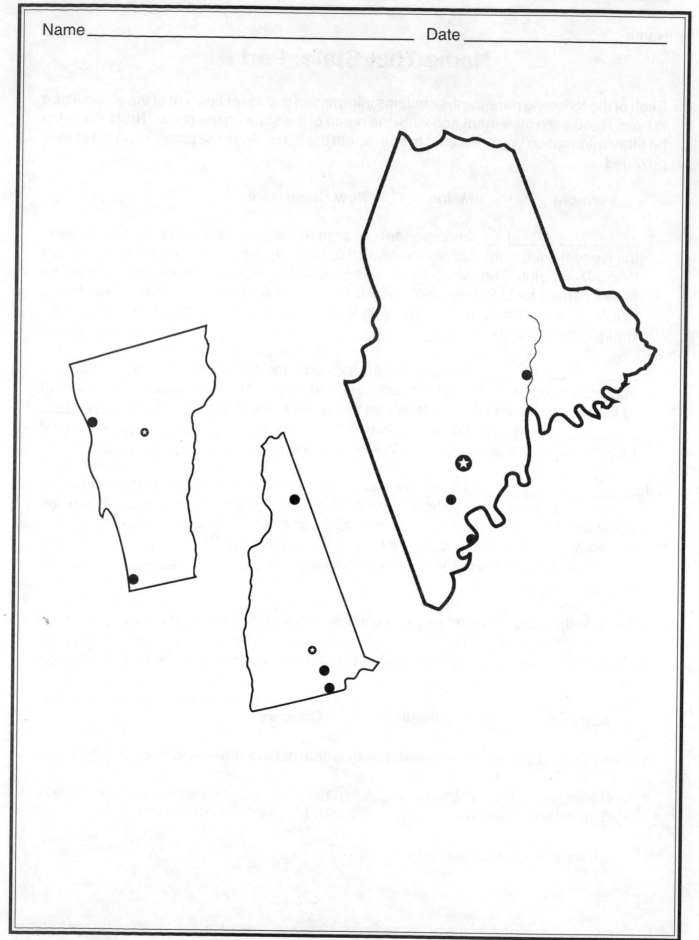

Name_____ Date _____

Name That State: Part III

Each of the following paragraphs contains information that identifies one of the states listed in bold. Read each statement and write the name of the state on the blank. There may also be other information you are asked to fill in about the state. Write the answers on the blanks provided.

Minnesota   **Iowa**   **Missouri**

1. _____ The name of this state comes from a Dakota Sioux word meaning "cloudy water." The nickname for the state is "The North Star State," and it entered the Union May 11, 1858. The capital, located on the headwaters of the Mississippi River, is known as one of the "twin cities." In this land of many lakes, water sports such as fishing are popular. The largest lake is Lake Superior, the largest of the Great Lakes. Many of the early settlers were from the northern European countries of Sweden and Norway. The neighbor to the north is Canada. The capital city is
a) _____ .

2. _____ This state has major rivers on its eastern and western borders. The name of the state is an Indian word that means "beautiful land." Neighbors to the west include Nebraska and South Dakota. This state is an important agricultural state, producing large amounts of corn and soybeans. This state is known as "The Hawkeye State." The capital is a) _____ . The river that forms the eastern border is the b) _____ River. The river that forms the western boundary is the c) _____ River.

3. _____ After the United States completed the Louisiana Purchase, President Jefferson commissioned Lewis and Clark to explore this newly purchased land. Lewis and Clark began their exploration from a city in this state. This city, located on the Mississippi River, has the famous "Gateway Arch." The state name is an Indian word that means "People of the Big Canoes." The famous Santa Fe and Oregon trails began near the city of Independence. The Ozark Plateau is an important physical feature found in this state. The capital city is a)_____ . The city on the Mississippi where Lewis and Clark began their exploration trip up the Missouri River is b)_____ .

4. Refer to the state maps on page 18 and locate Missouri, Minnesota, and Iowa.

5. Place the name of each of the following capital cities by the dot on the map that locates the city.

   St. Paul   **Jefferson City**   **Des Moines**

Name_____ Date _____

6. Place the name of the city on the map by the dot that locates each of the following cities.

St. Louis   **Council Bluffs**   **Waterloo**   **Hannibal**   **International Falls**
Duluth   **Minneapolis**   **Rochester**   **Burlington**   **Kansas City**

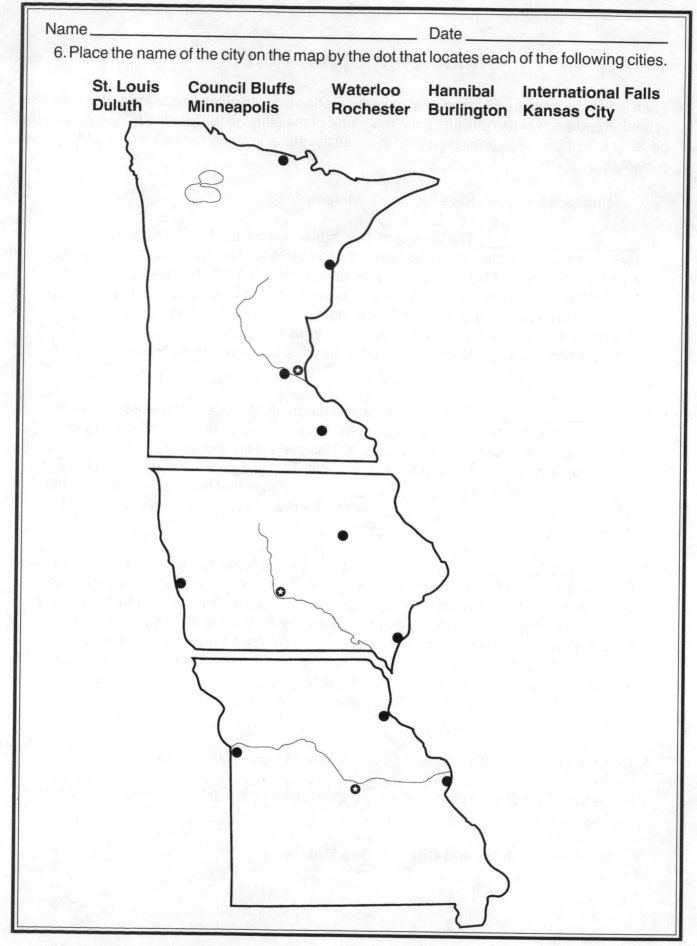

Name _____   Date _____

Name That State: Part IV

Each of the following paragraphs contains information that identifies one of the states listed in bold. Read each statement and write the name of the state on the blank. There may also be other information you are asked to fill in about the state. Write the answers on the blanks provided.

Oregon   **Washington**   **Idaho**

1. _____ Known as the "Beaver State," the Cascade Mountains are an important physical feature of this state. Mt. Hood, a snowcapped volcanic peak, is over 11,000 feet high and is a fascinating feature. The Columbia River forms the border with the state to the north. Many settlers followed the Oregon Trail to settle here in the fertile Willamette Valley. The capital is a)_____ . The neighbor state to the east is b) _____ .

2. _____ Mt. Olympia, Mt. Saint Helens, and Mt. Rainier are examples of volcanic peaks in this state. Snowcapped, these peaks are important landmarks. The capital is located at the southern end of Puget Sound. This state is a neighbor to a Canadian province to the north. The capital is a) _____ . A major river is the b) _____ .

3. _____ The Snake River and Bitterroot Mountains are found in this state. Lead mining in the city of Coeur d'Alene has been very important to this state. Settlers following the Oregon Trail crossed this state as they migrated to the Oregon Territory. The Craters of the Moon national park is a large area of lava fields with rounded cylinders and black glassy volcanic stone that tells a story of extensive volcanic activity that occurred 5,000 to 10,000 years ago. The capital is a)_____ . An important river is the b)_____ .

4. Refer to the state maps on page 20 and locate Oregon, Washington, and Idaho.

5. Place the name of each of the following capital cities by the dot on the map that locates the city.

   Olympia   **Boise**   **Salem**

6. Place the name of the city on the map by the dot that locates each of the following cities.

   Seattle   **Walla Walla**   **Pocatello**   **Klamath Falls**
   Eugene   **Spokane**   **Coeur d'Alene**   **Twin Falls**

Name_____ Date _____

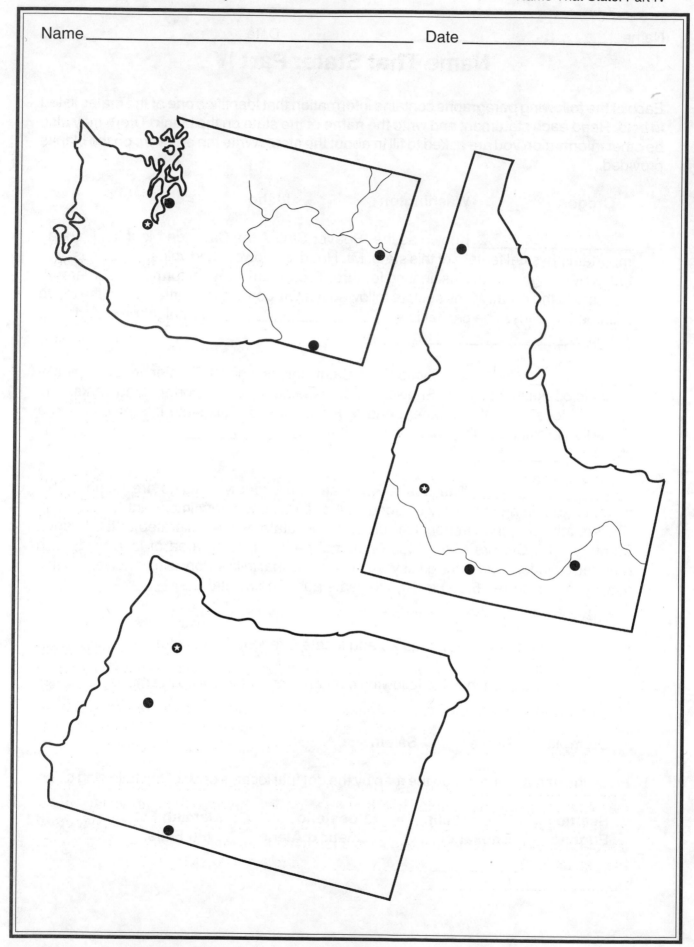

Name _____ Date _____

Name That State: Part V

Each of the following paragraphs contains information that identifies one of the states listed in bold. Read each statement and write the name of the state on the blank. There may also be other information you are asked to fill in about the state. Write the answers on the blanks provided.

Pennsylvania　　　**New Jersey**　　　**Delaware**　　　**Connecticut**

1. _____ Known as "The Garden State," this state with a population density of over 1,000 people per square mile is the most densely-populated state. One of the Middle Atlantic states, trucking, farming, dairying, and poultry farming are very important. This was the third state admitted to the Union. On Christmas night, 1776, General George Washington and his soldiers rowed across the Delaware River to attack the British at Trenton. Washington and his soldiers surprised the Hessian soldiers and captured weapons and supplies. The capital is a)_____. The Delaware River forms the border between this state and b) _____ .

2. _____ In this state, the oil industry began in 1859 when two men known as Uncle Billy Smith and Colonel Drake struck oil at Titusville. Known as the "Quaker State," it is also the home of Independence Hall, where the Declaration of Independence was signed. The Allegheny Mountains are an important physical feature, as are the Allegheny and Monongahela Rivers, which join the Ohio River. A famous Civil War battle was fought at Gettysburg, where 42,000 soldiers lost their lives. President Lincoln would later deliver the famous Gettysburg Address at the same site. The nickname is "The Keystone State." The capital is a)_____ . An important iron- and steel-producing city located where the Monongahela and Allegheny Rivers enter the Ohio River is b)_____ . The c) _____ River empties into Delaware Bay. The city of d) _____ is known as "The City of Brotherly Love" and was the site of the Constitutional Convention.

3. _____ This is the second smallest state in the United States in area. The largest city is Wilmington, which is not the capital. Cross a bay by the same name as the state and one is in New Jersey. This state is located on a peninsula that it shares with Maryland, and it finds the Chesapeake Bay on the west and the Delaware Bay on the east. Dover, the capital, is located in the northern part of the state. This was the first state to ratify the U.S. Constitution and the first to be admitted to the Union.

4. _____ Known as "The Constitution State," Puritans from Massachusetts came to this state to settle and farm the rich land found in the river valley known by the same name as the state. The neighbor state to the east is the smallest state in area. The southern border of the state is a famous harbor across which is Long Island. The capital is a)_____ . The fertile river valley is the b)_____ .

21

Name _____ Date _____

5. Locate Connecticut, New Jersey, Pennsylvania, and Delaware on the state maps below.

6. Place the name of the following capital cities by the dot on the map that locates each city.

| **Harrisburg** | **Dover** | **Trenton** | **Hartford** |

7. Place the name of the city on the map by the dot that locates each of the following cities.

Atlantic City	**New Haven**	**Philadelphia**	**Erie**
Wilmington	**Newark**	**Bristol**	**Harrington**
Pittsburgh	**Seaford**	**Bridgeport**	**Camden**

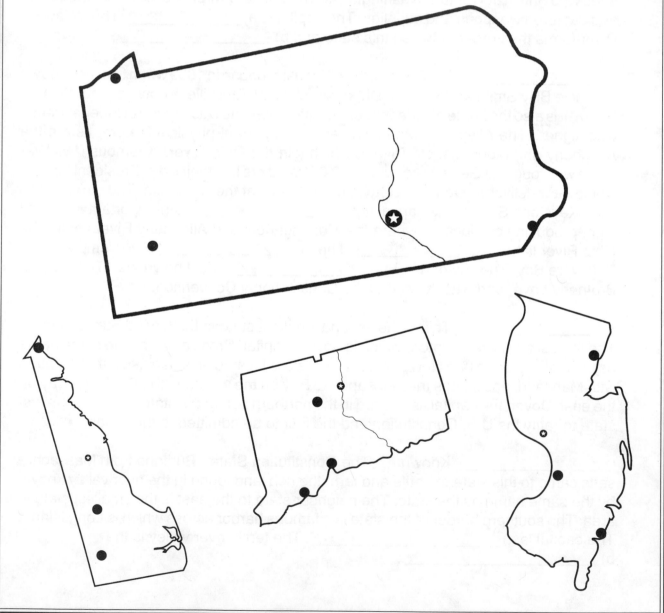

Name_____ Date _____

Name That State: Part VI

Each of the following paragraphs contains information that identifies one of the states listed in bold. Read each statement and write the name of the state on the blank.

Alaska   **Hawaii**

1._____ This was the last state to enter the union. It is a group of islands in the Pacific Ocean. The Battle of Pearl Harbor occurred in this state during World War II. Mauna Loa is one of the active volcanoes in this state.

2._____ This state is separated from the rest of the United States by Canada. It was the site of a Gold Rush in the Klondike region in 1897. The purchase of this territory from Russia in 1867 was called "Seward's Folly."

3. Locate Alaska and Hawaii on the state maps below.

4. Place the name of the following capital cities by the dot on the map that locates each city.

   Juneau   **Honolulu**

5. Place the name of the city on the map by the dot that locates each of the following cities.

Hilo	**Anchorage**	**Valdez**	**Wailuku**
Lihue	**Wahiawa**	**Fairbanks**	**Barrow**

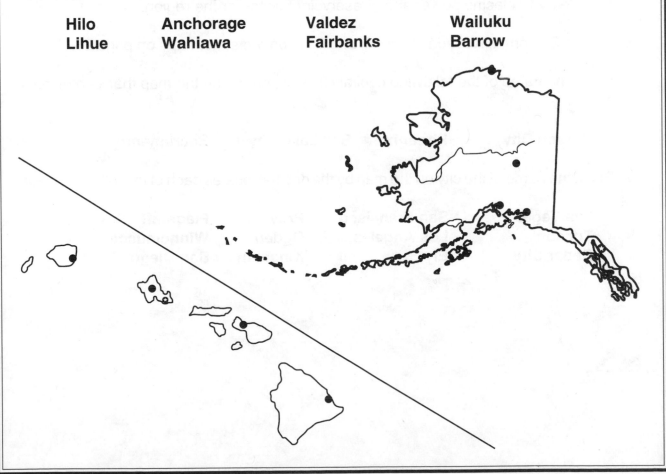

Name_____ Date _____

Name That State: Part VII

Each of the following paragraphs contains information that identifies one of the states listed in bold. Read each statement and write the name of the state on the blank.

California   Nevada   Arizona   Utah

1. _____ This state contains the Grand Canyon, which was formed by the Colorado River. Several Native American reservations are also located in the state. The capital is Phoenix.

2. _____ Mountain ranges in this state include the Sierra Nevada, the Cascade Range, and the Coast Ranges. When gold was discovered near Sutter's Mill in this state, it triggered the Gold Rush of 1849.

3. _____ Members of the Mormon Church were the first to settle this territory. They called their state Deseret until it was admitted to the union in 1896. The capital is Salt Lake City, which is near the Great Salt Lake.

4. _____ People visiting this state can gamble legally in cities such as Las Vegas and Reno. The Hoover Dam was built on the Colorado River in this state to provide hydroelectric power and a reservoir of water for the region.

5. Locate California, Nevada, Arizona, and Utah on the state maps on page 25.

6. Place the name of the following capital cities by the dot on the map that locates each city.

   Carson City   Phoenix   Salt Lake City   Sacramento

7. Place the name of the city on the map by the dot that locates each of the following cities.

Las Vegas	**San Francisco**	**Provo**	**Flagstaff**
Tucson	**Los Angeles**	**Ogden**	**Winnemucca**
Cedar City	**Ely**	**Kingman**	**San Diego**

Name _____ Date _____

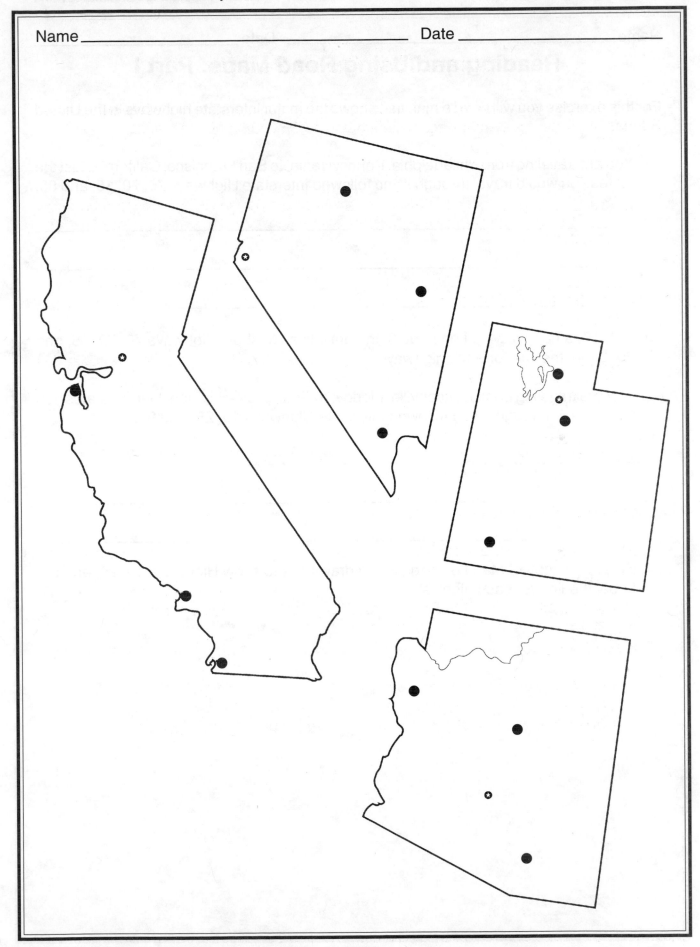

Name_____ Date _____

Reading and Using Road Maps: Part I

For this exercise you will need a map that shows the major interstate highways in the United States.

1. You are traveling from Philadelphia, Pennsylvania, to San Francisco, California. List the states you would travel through if you followed Interstate Highways 76, 70, 15, and 80.

_____

_____

_____

2. Refer to a copy of Map I on page 3 and draw lines to show Highways 76, 70, 15, and 80. Label the line for each highway.

3. You are traveling from Jacksonville, Florida, to Seattle, Washington. List the states you would pass through if you followed Interstate Highways 10, 25, and 90.

_____

_____

_____

4. Refer to a copy of Map I on page 3 and draw lines to show Highways 10, 25, and 90. Label the line for each highway.

Name _____ Date _____

Reading and Using Road Maps: Part II

For this exercise you will need a map that shows the major interstate highways in the United States. Refer to the map and solve the following situations/problems.

1. **Situation:** The year is 1803 and Meriwether Lewis and William Clark have been commissioned by President Thomas Jefferson to explore the newly acquired Louisiana Purchase. Lewis and Clark intend to leave on the exploration from St. Louis, Missouri, go up the Missouri River, and proceed to the Pacific Ocean.

   Problem: Refer to the map that shows the present-day interstate highways and assume the highways and states were there when Lewis and Clark began their journey. On the blanks below, indicate the **highways** and **states** they might have traversed to complete their exploration. (Remember, they wanted to follow the Missouri River as much as possible. Refer to an American history text, an encyclopedia, or some other source to see the route of the Lewis-and-Clark expedition.)

   _____

   _____

   _____

   _____

2. **Situation:** The year is 1846 and settlers are pressing west. Most are leaving from Independence, Missouri. Some are going northwest to the Oregon Territory, while others are going southwest to California. Some groups are following the Oregon Trail, while the others are following the Santa Fe Trail.

   Problem: You are part of a group that is going to California. You will follow the Santa Fe Trail to Santa Fe and then take the Old Spanish Trail into Utah and then the Salt Lake to Los Angeles Trail into California. Refer to your map and determine the **highways** and **states** you would use to most closely follow these trails. (Refer to an American history text, an encyclopedia, or some other source to see the route of the western trails.)

   _____

   _____

   _____

   _____

Name _____ Date _____

Map Measurements

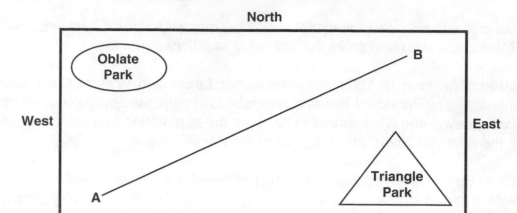

North

Oblate Park

B

West   East

Triangle Park

A

South   One inch equals 100 miles.

There is a country known as "Rectangle Land," shown above. Refer to the map of Rectangle Land and answer the following questions.

1. The western boundary of Rectangle Land is _____ miles from north to south.

2. The southern boundary of Rectangle Land is _____ miles from east to west.

3. Oblate Park is located in the a) southeast b) southwest c) northeast d) northwest corner of Rectangle Land.

4. Oblate Park is _____ miles wide from east to west at the widest point.

5. The area of Rectangle Land is a) 60,000 b) 12,000 c) 9,750 d) 85,000 square miles.

6. The distance from "A" to "B" is _____ miles.

7. Triangle Park is located in the a) southeast b) southwest c) northeast d) northwest.

8. The distance in miles around the border of Rectangle Land is _____ miles.

Many times a map will measure distance in kilometers rather than miles. A mile equals 1.6 kilometers. Another way of comparing a mile to a kilometer is to say a kilometer is 0.66 of a mile. On a map scale, the comparison might read: 1 mile = 1.6 kilometers. Ten miles would equal 10 x 1.6 = 16 kilometers. Complete the following table and change miles to kilometers.

Miles x 1.6 = Kilometers		Miles x 1.6 = Kilometers	
9.	1 x 1.6 = _____ km	10.	10 x 1.6 = _____ km
11.	100 x 1.6 = _____ km	12.	1,000 x 1.6 = _____ km

13. The distance in kilometers from Point A to Point B on the map of Rectangle Land is _____ kilometers.

14. The eastern boundary of Rectangle Land from north to south is _____ kilometers.

15. The northern boundary of Rectangle Land from east to west is _____ kilometers.

16. The distance in kilometers around Rectangle Land is _____ kilometers.

Name_____ Date _____

Size of the United States Compared to Other Nations

Population and People

The United States is one of the world's largest nations in population. The 10 largest nations in population are listed below. Refer to Chart I and complete the following exercise.

1. Rank the nations from largest to smallest by placing the numbers one through 10 on the blanks.

Chart I

Country	Population	Rank
a. Nigeria	89,000,000	_____
b. China	1,227,000,000	_____
c. Russia	148,000,000	_____
d. Indonesia	199,000,000	_____
e. Japan	125,000,000	_____
f. United States	264,000,000	_____
g. Brazil	161,000,000	_____
h. India	943,000,000	_____
i. Pakistan	144,000,000	_____
j. Bangladesh	118,000,000	_____

Total: _____

2. The United States is number _____ in population size.

3. The total population represented by the nations on the chart is _____ .

Name _____ Date _____

Using Graphs to Show Information

Circle Graphs

Information is often displayed in graphs to make it more meaningful. One kind of graph is the circle or pie graph. In this kind of graph, the total area of the circle represents the entire amount of data that is being graphed. For example, the population of the 10 largest nations of the world is approximately 3,418,000,000. The circle Graph A below represents this total number of 3,418,000,000. The entire Graph A represents 100 percent of the population of the 10 largest nations. Circle Graph B also represents the total population of these nations. However, the small, darkly-shaded pie piece of the circle represents the percent of the population of the 10 largest nations of the world that lives in the United States.

Graph A

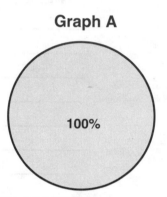

100%

Population of the 10 Largest Nations

Graph B

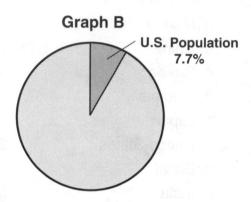

U.S. Population 7.7%

Population of the 10 Largest Nations

To determine the percentage part of a circle graph, divide the amount of the wedge by the amount of the total. Then you must remember that the total circle is 360 degrees. To determine the size of the piece of pie for each piece of data, you must multiply the percentage that the piece represents times 360 degrees. That number of degrees is then marked on the circle to represent the desired data.

Example: The total area of the circle in Graph C represents the population of the United States. California's population is 36 million or 14 percent of the total U.S. population.

California pop. ÷ U.S. pop. = 0.14 = 14%   14% * 360 degrees = 50 degrees

Fifty degrees marked on Graph C represents California's population as a part of the total U.S. population.

Graph C: U.S. Population

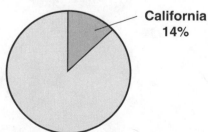

California 14%

30

Name_____ Date_____

Refer to Chart II below and complete the following.

1. Find the percentage that each nation's population is of the total. Place the percentage on the blank by the name of each nation.

Chart II

Country	Population	Percent of Total	Degrees Represented on Circle
a. Nigeria	89,000,000	_____	_____
b. China	1,227,000,000	_____	_____
c. Russia	148,000,000	_____	_____
d. Indonesia	199,000,000	_____	_____
e. Japan	125,000,000	_____	_____
f. United States	264,000,000	_____	_____
g. Brazil	161,000,000	_____	_____
h. India	943,000,000	_____	_____
i. Pakistan	144,000,000	_____	_____
j. Bangladesh	118,000,000	_____	_____
Total:	3,418,000,000	= 100 %	= 360 Degrees

Each of graphs D, E, F, G, and H represents the population for a nation in Chart II compared to the total population of the 10 largest nations. Complete each of the graphs D, E, F, G, and H to show the following comparisons.

2. On Graph D, show the population of the United States when compared to the total population shown on Chart II.
3. On Graph E, show the population of China when compared to the total population shown on Chart II.
4. On Graph F, show the population of India when compared to the total population shown on Chart II.
5. On Graph G, show the population of Brazil when compared to the total population shown on Chart II.
6. On Graph H, show the population of Nigeria when compared to the total population shown on Chart II.

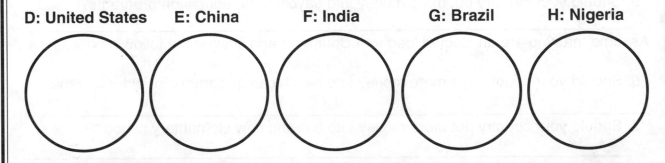

D: United States   E: China   F: India   G: Brazil   H: Nigeria

Name_____ Date _____

Learning About Population Pyramids

It is important to know the percentage of population represented by each age group in a nation. One method of graphically studying the different age groups is with a population pyramid. The population pyramids below are examples that show the percentage of the population for various age groups in two different countries. Note in reading the population pyramid that the base shows the percentage that each group is of the total. For example, in Country A, 0–9 age group is 24 percent of the population. The population pyramid also shows the percent of males and females for each age group.

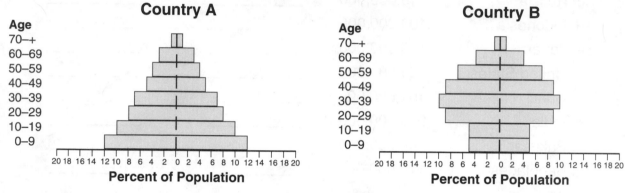

Note that the population pyramids for Country A and Country B are much different. Refer to the population pyramids for Country A and Country B and answer the following questions.

1. The country with a population pyramid that is shaped like a Christmas tree is
    a) Country A   b) Country B.

2. The population pyramid with a large percentage of younger people and a small percentage of older people is   a) Country A   b) Country B.

3. The population pyramid that shows people living longer and making up a larger part of the population is   a) Country A   b) Country B.

Population pyramids can be used by the leaders in a country to make plans for the future. Assume that you are an elected leader of Country A and answer the following questions.

4. Should your country put more money into building new nursing homes?

_____

5. Should your country put more money into daycare and education programs?

_____

Assume that you are an elected leader of Country B and answer the following questions.

6. Should your country put more money into health care programs for older citizens?

_____

7. Should your country put more money into building new elementary schools?

_____

Name_____ Date _____

Line and Bar Graphs and Population Trends

The line graph below shows the population growth of the United States. Complete the activities below the graph.

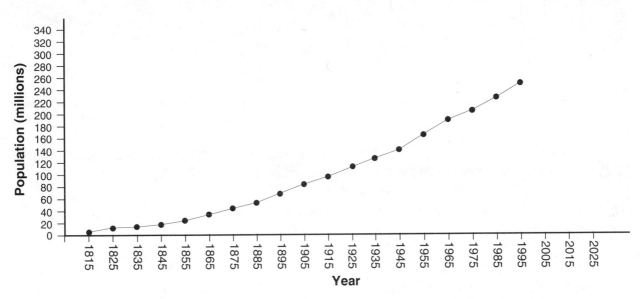

Population of the United States

1. Place dots to project the population for the years 2005, 2015, and 2025.

2. The following chart shows the populations of 10 states rounded to the nearest one hundred thousand. Use the population data in the chart and complete the following bar graph.

Chart A:	**State**	**Population**
	California	34,000,000
	Texas	19,500,000
	New York	18,800,000
	Florida	14,500,000
	Illinois	11,900,000
	New Mexico	1,800,000
	Montana	900,000
	South Dakota	700,000
	North Dakota	600,000
	Wyoming	500,000

Graph A: **Populations of Selected States**

Name_____ Date _____

Graph A: **Populations of Selected States**

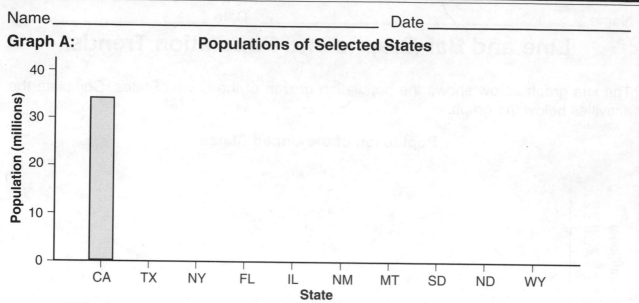

At the present rate of growth, the U.S. Census Bureau estimates that the population of the United States will increase by nine percent by the year 2010.

Refer to the map below and complete the following activities.

3. Color Texas, California, New Mexico, Nevada, Utah, and Arizona red. The population of these states is expected to increase 15 to 18 percent.

Name_____ Date _____

4. Column I in Chart B below shows the populations of these states. Increase the population of each state by 16 percent and write the new population number on the blank in Column II. This figure in Column II is the projected population of each state in 2010.

Chart B:	State	Column I	Column II
	Texas	19,500,000	_____
	California	34,000,000	_____
	Arizona	4,500,000	_____
	New Mexico	1,800,000	_____
	Nevada	1,700,000	_____
	Utah	2,100,000	_____

5. Complete the bar graph to show the increase in population for each state in Chart B for the 10-year period from 2000 to 2010.

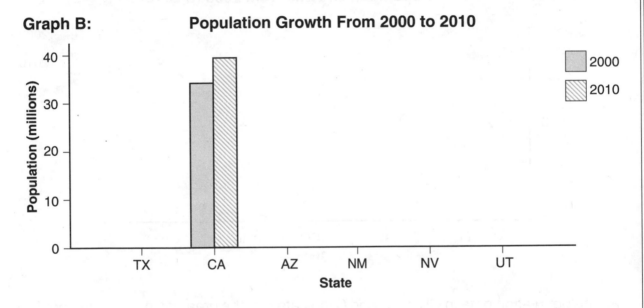

Graph B: Population Growth From 2000 to 2010

6. On the map on page 34, color Florida, Alabama, Colorado, Idaho, and Oregon brown. The population of these states will increase by 10 to 14 percent by the year 2010.

Name_____ Date _____

7. Column I in Chart C shows the population for these states. Increase the population of each state by 13 percent and write the new population number on the blank in Column II. This figure is the projected population of each state in 2010.

Chart C:	State	Column I	Column II
	Florida	14,500,000	_____
	Alabama	4,400,000	_____
	Colorado	4,100,000	_____
	Idaho	1,200,000	_____
	Oregon	3,300,000	_____

8. Complete the bar graph below to show the increase in population for each state in Chart C for the 10-year period from 2000 to 2010.

Graph C:

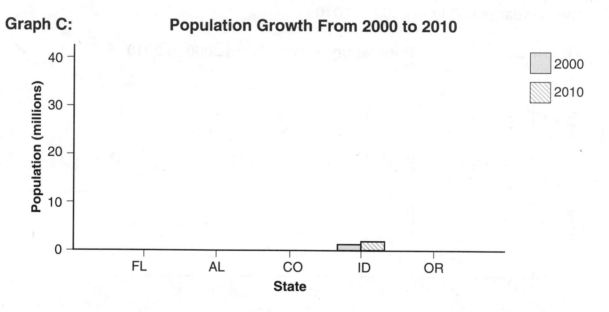

Population Growth From 2000 to 2010

9. The population data in Charts B and C indicate that the greatest increase in population in the United States will be in

a) the south and east.   b) the southwest and southeast.

c) the midwest and northeast.   d) the southwest and northwest.

Name_____ Date _____

Population Density

   Population density refers to the number of people who live in a specific area. The rectangle below represents a country called Goodland. The total population is 100,000. The area is 100 square miles. Each square represents a state in Goodland.

Goodland

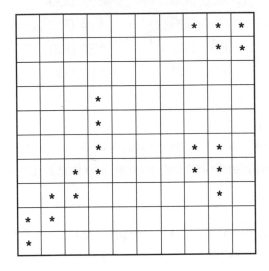

1. To find the average population density in Goodland, divide the population (100,000) by the area (100 square miles).

   a. 100,000 ÷ 100 = _____

   b. So the population density per square mile in Goodland is _____.

2. Population density is not usually evenly distributed in a nation. For example, in Goodland, 50,000 of the 100,000 people live in the 20 states with the symbol *. Each state in Goodland has an area of one square mile. To find the population of the 20 states, divide the population (50,000) by the area (20 square miles).

   a. 50,000 ÷ 20 = _____

   b. So the population density for these 20 states in Goodland is _____ people per square mile.

3. The average population density in the remaining 80 states in Goodland is _____ people per square mile.

Name_____ Date _____

4. The chart below shows the population and area for Texas, Arizona, New Mexico, Nevada, and Utah. For each state, divide the population by the area to find the population density per square mile. Write the population density on the blank under that column.

State	Population	Area (Square Miles)	Population Density
a. Texas	19,500,000	267,000	_____
b. Arizona	4,500,000	114,000	_____
c. New Mexico	1,800,000	122,000	_____
d. Nevada	1,700,000	111,000	_____
e. Utah	2,100,000	85,000	_____

5. The state with the greatest population density per square mile is _____.

6. The states with the smallest population density per square mile are_____ and_____.

7. The chart below shows the population and area for 10 world nations. Find the population density for each nation and write it on the blank.

Nation	Population	Area (Square Miles)	Population Density	Rank
a. Nigeria	89,000,000	357,000	_____	_____
b. China	1,227,000,000	3,705,000	_____	_____
c. Russia	148,000,000	6,593,000	_____	_____
d. Indonesia	199,000,000	735,000	_____	_____
e. Japan	125,000,000	146,000	_____	_____
f. United States	264,000,000	3,619,000	_____	_____
g. Brazil	161,000,000	3,286,000	_____	_____
h. India	943,000,000	1,269,000	_____	_____
i. Pakistan	144,000,000	307,000	_____	_____
j. Bangladesh	118,000,000	56,000	_____	_____

8. The country with the greatest population density per square mile is_____.

9. The country with the smallest population density per square mile is_____.

10. Write each country's rank in population density on the blank labeled Rank.

Name_____ Date_____

Elevation and Contour Maps

Diagram A:

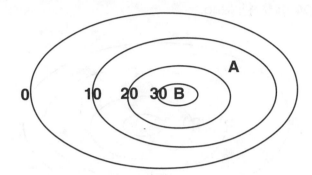

    Assume that Diagram A is an island located in the Pacific Ocean. The lines shown on the map are contour lines. Contour lines are lines that connect all the points that are the same elevation above sea level. In Diagram A, the contour lines are labeled 0, 10, 20, and 30. The contour line representing zero is at sea level. Sea level is the point where the land of the island meets the ocean. The contour line labeled 10 is 10 feet above sea level. The contour lines labeled 20 and 30 mark points that are 20 and 30 feet above sea level.

    The spacing of the contour lines shows how steep or level the land is. The closer the contour lines are, the steeper the land. Widely-spaced contour lines indicate that the land is level.

    Many maps show the elevation by using different colors. For example, green is often used to show lower elevations, while brown shades are used to show higher elevations. Understanding contour maps will help you understand how maps showing elevation are developed.

Refer to Diagram A and complete the following.

1. Color the part of the island between the contour lines representing 0 and 10 feet above sea level light green.
2. Color the part of the island between the contour lines representing 10 and 20 feet above sea level dark green.
3. Color the part of the island between the contour lines representing 20 and 30 feet above sea level light brown.
4. Color the part of the island above the contour line representing 30 feet above sea level dark brown.

5. Point A is at an elevation that is   a) between 10 and 20 feet

    b) between 20 and 30 feet   c) between 0 and 10 feet   above sea level.

6. Point B is at an elevation that is   a) above 30 feet   b) between 20 and 30 feet

    c) between 10 and 20 feet   d) below 10 feet   above sea level.

Name_____ Date _____

Many times maps that show elevation will have a cross section profile that shows a profile of the mapped area. For example, Diagram A is shown below with a cross section profile to show the shape of the island.

Diagram A:

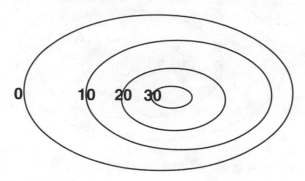

40 ft. above sea level _____

30 ft. above sea level _____

20 ft. above sea level _____

10 ft. above sea level _____

0 ft. above sea level _____

Diagram B below is an island near the island represented by Diagram A. Refer to Diagram B and complete the activity below.

Diagram B:

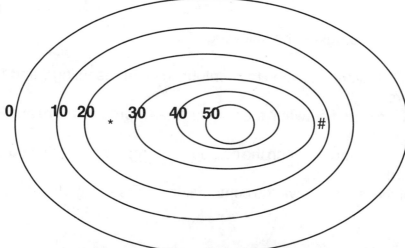

7. Color the area between the 0- and 10-foot contour lines light green. Color each area progressively darker green up to the 30-foot line.

8. Color the area between the 30- and 40-foot contour lines light brown. Color each area progressively darker brown up to the 50-foot line.

9. Color the area inside the 50-foot contour line very dark brown.

10. Is the symbol # or * located at a steeper part of the island? _____

Name_____ Date _____

11. In the space below, tell the reason for your answer to question 10.

_____

_____

Follow the directions below to create a cross section profile of the island in Diagram B.

12. Draw a line from Point A on the 0 ft. line to Point B on the 10 ft. line.
13. Draw a line from Point B on the 10 ft. line to Point C on the 20 ft. line.
14. Draw a line from Point C on the 20 ft. line to Point D on the 30 ft. line.
15. Draw a line from Point D on the 30 ft. line to Point E on the 40 ft. line.
16. Draw a line from Point E on the 40 ft. line to Point F on the 50 ft. line.
17. Draw a line from Point F on the 50 ft. line to Point G on the 50 ft. line.
18. Draw a line from Point G on the 50 ft. line to Point H on the 40 ft. line.
19. Draw a line from Point H on the 40 ft. line to Point I on the 30 ft. line.
20. Draw a line from Point I on the 30 ft. line to Point J on the 20 ft. line.
21. Draw a line from Point J on the 20 ft. line to Point K on the 10 ft. line.
22. Draw a line from Point K on the 10 ft. line to Point L on the 0 ft. line.

Each point in the cross section profile is directly below the farthest extent of a line on the contour map in Diagram B (see dashed line). By connecting the dots, you have made a profile outline of how steep the land is on the island.

Diagram B:

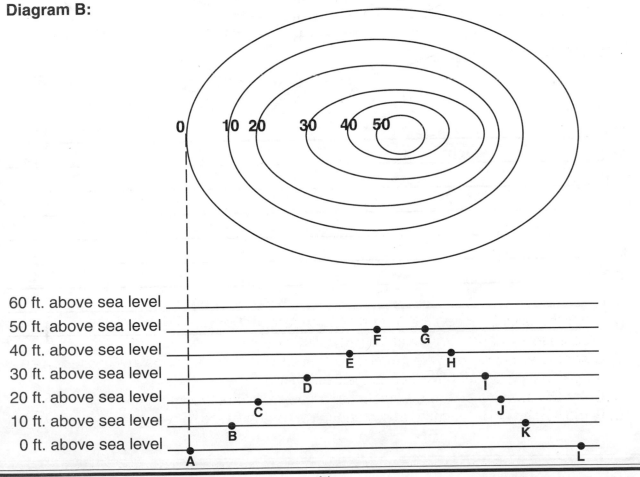

Name_____ Date _____

More Elevation Practice

1. Refer to Diagram C and create a cross section profile of the island on the lines below the diagram.

Diagram C:

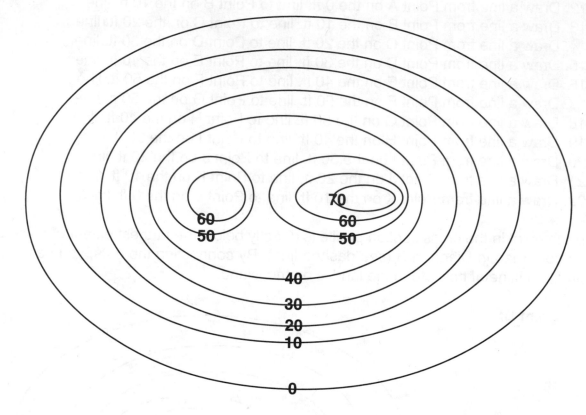

80 ft. _____

70 ft. _____

60 ft. _____

50 ft. _____

40 ft. _____

30 ft. _____

20 ft. _____

10 ft. _____

0 ft. _____

42

Name_____ Date _____

Understanding Temperature Maps

Many daily newspapers include weather maps that show the daily weather conditions in various parts of the United States. These maps use colors to show temperature conditions that will exist in various parts of the United States on a given day.

The temperature bands (colored zones) are developed by drawing isotherms on the map and coloring the temperature areas between the bands. For example, on the map below, each dot represents the temperature listed by the dot. **Isotherms** are lines connecting places with the same temperature. **Iso = equal** and **therm = temperature**.

1. Use a pencil and draw a line connecting the dots that have the same temperatures on the map below. When you have connected the lines for each set of temperatures, you will have developed an isothermal map. The line connecting the dots with the same temperature is called an isotherm. Each isotherm has been started for you.

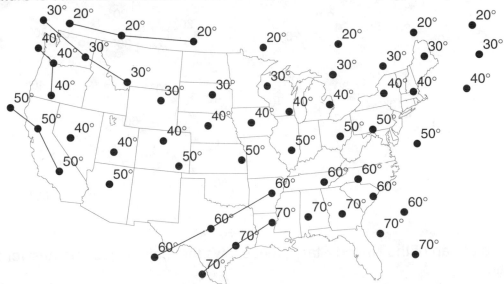

2. Color brown the area between the isotherm lines for 60 degrees and 70 degrees.
3. Color yellow the area between the isotherm lines for 50 degrees and 60 degrees.
4. Color blue the area between the isotherm lines for 40 degrees and 50 degrees.
5. Color purple the area between the isotherm lines for 30 degrees and 40 degrees.
6. Color pink the area between the isotherm lines for 20 degrees and 30 degrees.

Refer to a map of the United States that shows the major cities and the map above and answer the following questions.

7. List five cities that have a temperature between 60 and 70 degrees on the day shown in the map above.

_____

8. List five cities that have a temperature between 50 and 60 degrees.

_____

Name_____ Date _____

9. List five cities that have a temperature between 40 and 50 degrees.

_____

10. List five cities that have a temperature between 30 and 40 degrees.

_____

11. List five cities that have a temperature between 20 and 30 degrees.

_____

12. The map below shows the temperature for the United States a day later than the previous map. Use a pencil and connect the dots that have the same temperatures on the map.

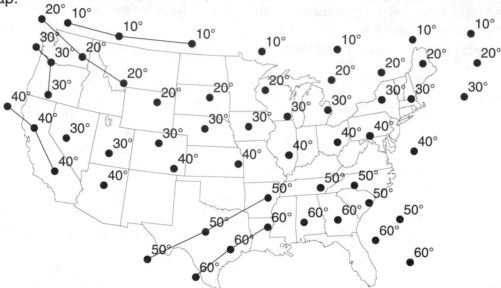

Refer to a map of the United States that shows the major cities and answer the following questions.

13. List five cities that have a temperature between 10 and 20 degrees on the day shown on the map above.

_____

14. List five cities that have a temperature above 60 degrees.

_____

15. List five cities that have a cooler temperature on the map above than on the map on page 43.

_____

_____

Name_____ Date _____

The Government of the United States

When the framers of the Constitution of the United States wrote the Constitution, they were very concerned about who made the laws, who executed the laws, and who judged the laws. It was important to the framers that there were three separate branches of the government. The branches are known as the legislative branch, executive branch, and judicial branch.

Legislative Branch

All legislative powers shall be **vested** in a **Congress** of the United States, which shall consist of the **House of Representatives** and **Senate**.

1. The term *vested* means   a) provided   b) placed   c) dressed.
2. The term *congress* means   a) vote   b) party   c) legislature.
3. Legislative power means the power to   a) make laws   b) judge laws   c) enforce laws.

The House of Representatives

Representatives shall be chosen every second year by the people of the several states. No person shall be a representative who has not **attained** the age of twenty-five years and been seven years a citizen of the United States, and who shall not when elected be an inhabitant of that state in which he shall be chosen.

4. The term *representatives* means   a) Senate members   b) House of Representatives members.
5. Representatives are chosen every a) year   b) three years   c) two years   d) six years.
6. Representatives of each state are chosen by   a) citizens of each state   b) the president.
7. The term *attained* means   a) to arrive at   b) to buy   c) to remain.

Representatives and direct taxes shall be **apportioned** among the several states according to their respective numbers. The actual **enumeration** shall be made within three years after the first meeting of Congress and every 10 years thereafter. Each state shall have no more than one representative for every 30,000 citizens. However, each state shall have at least one representative.

8. The term *apportioned* means   a) counted   b) divided   c) published.
9. The term *enumeration* means   a) count   b) question   c) speech.
10. Each state has one representative for every   a) 10   b) 30   c) 5   d) 100   thousand citizens.

Name_____ Date _____

11. Complete the following chart for the state in which you live.

State	Population	Number of Legislative Districts	Number of Legislators
_____	_____	_____	_____

12. The representative for the legislative district in which I live is a)_____
_____, who is a member of the   b)_____ Party.
He/She has been a representative for c) _____ years, or d)_____
terms.

13. The following table shows the population of 10 states. The population is rounded to the nearest hundred thousand.

The state with the most representatives is a)_____ because
b) _____

_____ .

The state with the fewest representatives is c)_____ because
d) _____

_____ .

State	Population
1. California	32,500,000
2. Texas	19,500,000
3. New York	18,200,000
4. Florida	14,700,000
5. Illinois	11,900,000
6. New Mexico	1,700,000
7. Montana	900,000
8. South Dakota	700,000
9. North Dakota	600,000
10. Wyoming	500,000

Name_____ Date _____

House of Representatives Review

Complete each blank using one of the following terms.

seven   **Congress**   **attained**   **inhabitant**   **legislative**
twenty-five **chosen**   **vested**   **citizen**

    All (1)_____ powers shall be (2)_____ in a (3)_____ of the United States, which shall consist of the House of Representatives and Senate. Representatives shall be (4)_____ every second year by the people of the several states. No person shall be a representative who has not (5)_____ the age of (6)_____ years and been (7)_____ years a (8)_____ of the United States, and who shall not when elected be an (9)_____ of that state in which he shall be chosen.

Read the following selections and decide if the person qualifies to run for the House of Representatives

10. John Jones is 25 years old. He was born in Ireland and came to the United States when he was five years of age. He became a citizen at the age of 21. He owns a farm in Vermont, but he lives in Massachusetts. John wants to be a candidate for the House of Representatives in Vermont. Is he eligible? Why or why not?

_____

_____

11. Sally Labou is 31 years of age. She was born in New York but now lives in Kentucky. She has lived in Kentucky for 10 years. Sally intends to become a candidate for the House of Representatives. Is she eligible? Why or why not?

_____

_____

12. Jose Rivera is 39 years of age and lives in Chicago, Illinois. He has been a citizen of the United States for five years. Jose intends to become a candidate for the House of Representatives in the next election, which is two years from now. Will he be eligible? Why or why not?

_____

_____

Name_____ Date _____

The Senate

Each state shall have two senators elected for six years. Each senator shall have one vote. One-third of the Senate is elected every two years. Each senator must be thirty years of age, a citizen of the United States for nine years, and an inhabitant of the state from which elected.

Using the terms below, complete the following blanks.

six   **nine**   **one**   **two**   **thirty**

Each state shall have (1)_____ senators elected for (2) _____ years. Each senator shall have (3)_____ vote. Each senator must be (4)_____ years of age, a citizen of the United States for (5) _____ years, and an inhabitant of the state from which elected.

The vice president of the United States shall be president of the Senate. However, the vice president shall not have a vote, except to break a tie vote among the senators. All impeachments shall be tried by the Senate. When the president of the United States is tried for impeachment, the chief justice of the Supreme Court presides over the trial in the Senate.

Using the terms below, complete the following blanks.

chief justice   **impeachments**   **Senate**   **tie**   **president**

The vice president of the United States shall be (6) _____ of the Senate. However, the vice president shall not have a vote, except to break a (7) _____ vote among the Senators. All (8) _____ shall be tried by the Senate. When the president of the United States is tried for impeachment, the (9) _____ _____ of the Supreme Court presides over the trial in the (10)_____.

Name_____ Date _____

Legislation

Congress, including the House of Representatives and the Senate, has the authority to propose legislation to raise revenue. Revenue bills originate in the House of Representatives. However, all such bills must be approved by the Senate. Many times a bill will be sent by the House of Representatives to the Senate. The Senate may amend the bill and return it to the House of Representatives. When the House of Representatives and the Senate agree on a revenue bill, it is then sent to the president. The president may choose to sign the bill and make it law. However, the president may veto the bill and send it back to Congress.

Using the terms below, complete the following blanks.

president   House of Representatives   Senate

Congress, including the (1) _____ and the (2)_____, has the authority to propose legislation to raise revenue. Revenue bills originate in the (3) _____. However, all such bills must be approved by the (4)_____. Many times a bill will be sent from the House of Representatives to the Senate. The Senate may amend the bill and return it to the House of Representatives. When the (5) _____ and the (6) _____ agree on a revenue bill, it is then sent to the (7) _____. The president may choose to sign the bill and make it law. However, the (8) _____ may veto the bill and send it back to Congress.

Match each definition in Column B with the correct term in Column A.

Column A	Column B
_____ 9. Legislation	A. Means having the right
_____ 10. Revenue	B. Means to change, correct, or improve
_____ 11. Impeachment	C. A member of a state or nation
_____ 12. Authority	D. Refers to making laws
_____ 13. Amend	E. One who lives in a state or country but may not be a citizen
_____ 14. Veto	F. Income for a state or country from taxation
_____ 15. Originate	G. To reject or prohibit
_____ 16. Inhabitant	H. Refers to the beginning or where first proposed
_____ 17. Citizen	I. To charge an officeholder with criminal activity and recommend a trial be held

Name _____ Date _____

The Executive Branch

   The executive powers of the Constitution are vested in the president of the United States. The president and vice president are elected for a term of four years. To be elected president, a candidate must be a natural-born U.S. citizen, at least thirty-five years of age, and a resident of the United States for 14 years.

   The president and vice president are elected by a group of electors from each state. The electors who choose the president and vice president are appointed in each state. These electors are known as the Electoral College. The number of electors appointed in each state equals the total number of senators and representatives for the individual states. However, no senator or representative who is serving in Congress may be appointed as a member of the Electoral College.

Answer the following questions. Select answers from the list below.

senators	four	Electoral College	representatives
executive	35	electors	

1. The power vested in the president is called the _____ power.

2. The president and vice president are elected for a term of _____ years.

3. To be a candidate for president or vice president, one must be _____ years of age.

4. The president and vice president are elected by _____ who are appointed in each state.

5. The electors appointed to cast votes for the president and vice president are known as the _____.

6. The number of members appointed to the Electoral College is determined by the number of _____ and _____ from each state.

Each of the following individuals wants to be a candidate for president or vice president. Read the listed qualifications and, on the blank below each description, write whether the individual could be elected president or vice president.

7. Jose Garcia is a natural-born citizen who lives in Texas. Jose is 33 years of age. If elected, he will be 34 years of age when he becomes president.

_____

8. Henry Jackson is 36 years of age and an immigrant from Ireland. He is living in Michigan and hopes to become a citizen of the United States.

_____

9. Nancy Molinski is 45 years of age. She was born in New York, but she now lives in Arizona.

_____

Name _____ Date _____

Read each of the following and determine if the individual is eligible to run for President, Vice President, Senator, or Representative. Indicate the offices the individual could be elected to on the blank below.

10. Sam Wright lives in California. He is 26 years of age and has been a citizen of the United States since he was 12 years old.

_____

_____

11. Maria Flores lives in Illinois. Maria was born in Chicago on December 12, 1964.

_____

_____

12. John Livingston is 86 years of age. He was born in Florida. John has lived in Oregon for the last seven years. Before moving to Oregon, John lived for 20 years in Mexico, working for a U.S. company and making fertilizer.

_____

_____

13. Hemshand Lumand is 39 years of age. Hemshand was born in Turkey. He came to the United States November 12, 1993. He is a medical doctor and works in a hospital in New York City. Hemshand intends to become a citizen of the United States.

_____

_____

Name_____ Date _____

Branches of the U.S. Government Crossword Puzzle

Use the clues below to complete the crossword puzzle about the U.S. government. You may need to refer to the material on pages 45 to 51 to find the answers.

ACROSS

1. Action by the president when a bill that the president does not want to become law is sent from the Congress
6. Number of members of the Supreme Court
10. One must be thirty-five to be elected to this office.
12. Refers to the power of the president
13. Age necessary to become a candidate for the Senate
15. Refers to the power of Congress

DOWN

2. Term of office for members of the House of Representatives (two words)
3. Term of office for the president and vice president (two words)
4. This person is also the president of the Senate (two words).
5. Refers to the power of the Supreme Court and lesser courts
7. Name given to the electors appointed to elect the president and vice president (two words)
8. The number of these members of Congress elected from a state depends on population.
9. Two are elected from each state.
11. Age necessary to become a candidate for the House of Representatives
14. Term of office for members of the Senate (two words)

       52

Name _____ Date _____

Electing the President and Vice President

The Electoral College

When the constitution of the United States was being written, the delegates from the 13 colonies did not want to leave the election of the president and vice president in the hands of the people, based on a popular vote. The framers of the constitution determined that each state would have an appointed Electoral College. Each state would appoint a group of people to the Electoral College, and this group would then elect the president and vice president. The number of members of the Electoral College in each state would be determined by the number of senators and representatives for the state.

The Popular Vote

Even though the president and vice president are elected by the Electoral College, every citizen who is eligible can vote for the president and vice president. Every four years, on the first Tuesday after the first Monday in November, the people of the United States vote for a president and vice president. Each individual who votes indicates his or her choice for president and vice president. This vote is referred to as the popular vote, because the people or "populace" cast their votes.

In each state, the names of the candidates receiving the most popular votes are submitted to the Electoral College. Each state has a specific number of electoral votes based on population. The members of the Electoral College then cast the electoral votes for each state for the president and vice president. The Electoral College members cast their votes for the candidates for president and vice president who receive the most popular votes in their state. So even though individual voters indicate their choice by the popular vote, it is the Electoral College in each state that actually casts the electoral votes for president and vice president. (It is possible that the people receiving the most popular votes would not be elected president and vice president. For example, in 1888, Grover Cleveland won the popular vote but, because he lost in the states with more electoral votes, lost the electoral vote to Benjamin Harrison.)

Name_____ Date _____

Electoral College Votes

The number of Electoral College votes for each state is determined by the number of senators and representatives that the state has in Congress. The number of electoral votes for each state are listed in the chart below.

Refer to the chart and complete the following activity.

1. The five states with the greatest number of electoral votes are _____, _____, _____, _____, and _____.

2. If a presidential candidate won the electoral votes for all five of the above states, the total would be _____ .

3. Any presidential and vice presidential candidates who receive _____ electoral votes are elected president and vice president.

Electoral College Votes for Individual States (The number required to elect a president is 270 votes.)

State	Population	Electoral Votes
Alabama	4,400,000	9
Alaska	615,000	3
Arizona	4,500,000	8
Arkansas	2,600,000	6
California	34,000,000	54
Colorado	4,100,000	8
Connecticut	3,270,000	8
Delaware	740,000	3
District of Columbia	530,000	3
Florida	14,500,000	25
Georgia	7,500,000	13
Hawaii	1,187,000	4
Idaho	1,210,000	4
Illinois	11,900,000	22
Indiana	5,900,000	12
Iowa	2,900,000	7
Kansas	2,600,000	6
Kentucky	3,950,000	8
Louisiana	4,400,000	9
Maine	1,250,000	4
Maryland	5,100,000	10
Massachusetts	6,150,000	12
Michigan	9,800,000	18
Minnesota	4,700,000	10

Name_____ Date _____

State	Population	Electoral Votes
Mississippi	2,775,000	7
Missouri	5,500,000	11
Montana	880,000	3
Nebraska	1,700,000	5
Nevada	1,700,000	4
New Hampshire	1,200,000	4
New Jersey	8,100,000	15
New Mexico	1,775,000	5
New York	18,800,000	33
North Carolina	7,000,000	14
North Dakota	600,000	3
Ohio	11,500,000	21
Oklahoma	3,500,000	8
Oregon	3,300,000	7
Pennsylvania	12,100,000	23
Rhode Island	990,000	4
South Carolina	3,800,000	8
South Dakota	735,000	3
Tennessee	5,400,000	11
Texas	19,500,000	32
Utah	2,100,000	5
Vermont	585,000	3
Virginia	6,800,000	13
Washington	5,650,000	11
West Virginia	1,820,000	5
Wisconsin	5,200,000	11
Wyoming	480,000	3
Total:	271,292,000	538

4. List the 10 states, in order, with the greatest number of electoral votes.

State	Votes
a. _____	_____
b. _____	_____
c. _____	_____
d. _____	_____
e. _____	_____
f. _____	_____
g. _____	_____
h. _____	_____
i. _____	_____
j. _____	_____

Name_____ Date _____

5. List the 10 largest states in population.

State	Population
a._____	_____
b._____	_____
c._____	_____
d._____	_____
e._____	_____
f._____	_____
g._____	_____
h._____	_____
i._____	_____
j._____	_____

Bar graphs are often used to show comparisions of data. A bar graph is a diagram that uses vertical or horizontal bars to visually represent the information compared. The vertical and horizontal sides of the diagram form coordinates that are used in determing the size of the bar for each item compared.

For example, in the diagram below, the horizontal side shows five states and the vertical side shows area in square miles. The coordinates for this chart are the points on the chart where a specific area in square miles on the vertical side meets a specific state on the horizontal side. For example, Texas is a specific coordinate on the horizontal side of the diagram and 262,000 square miles is the specific coordinate for the area of Texas on the vertical side of the diagram. Point A on the diagram is where the coordinates meet. The next step is to color in the bar graph.

6. Complete the bar graph for the other four states. A dot has been placed at the point where the top of each bar should be. Draw in the bars and color or shade them in.

Area of States

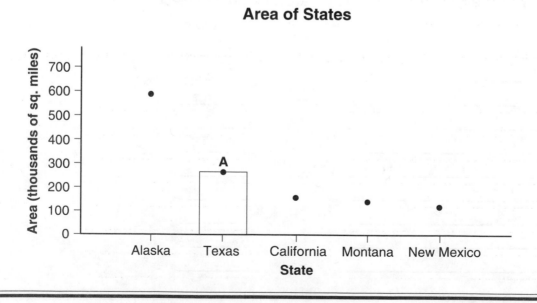

Name_____ Date _____

7. Complete the following to make a bar graph showing the 10 states with the greatest number of electoral votes. California has been completed for you.

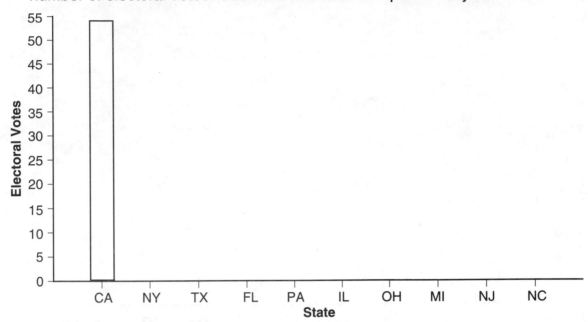

8. List the eight states with the smallest number of electoral votes in order from smallest to largest.

State   **Votes**

a._____   _____

b._____   _____

c._____   _____

d._____   _____

e._____   _____

f._____   _____

g._____   _____

h._____   _____

9. List the eight states with the smallest populations in order from smallest to largest.

State   **Population**

a._____   _____

b._____   _____

c._____   _____

d._____   _____

e._____   _____

f._____   _____

g._____   _____

h._____   _____

Name_____ Date _____

10. Complete the following to make a bar graph showing the eight states with the smallest populations. Wyoming has been completed for you.

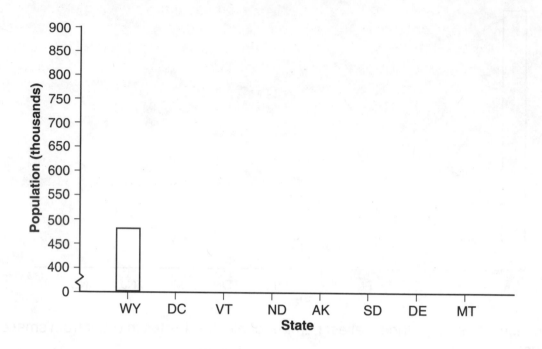

Refer to the graphs you have completed and answer the questions below.

11. T F   The total number of electoral votes needed to become president is 535.
12. T F   The number of electoral votes for each state is determined by the population of each state.
13. T F   The state with the greatest number of electoral votes is California.
14. T F   The total number of electoral votes for California, Texas, New York, Florida, and Pennsylvania is 167.
15. T F   An individual could be elected president by winning only the electoral votes for California, Texas, New York, Florida, and Pennsylvania.
16. The states below are growing at the rates indicated. If the growth continues, one would expect the number of electoral votes for each state to (increase/decrease) because

_____

_____

_____

Arizona (+3.0%), Colorado (+2.3%), Nevada (+4.6%), Utah (+2.5%)

Name _____ Date _____

U.S. Presidents

The period from 1789 to 1921 was a significant period in the history of the country. People were moving westward, new states were being added, conflict was developing among the states that would lead to a civil war, the nation was becoming more industrialized, and it was becoming a world leader. Below is a list of presidents who served during the period from 1789 to 1921. Each of the statements below relates to a U.S. president who served during this period. Read each of the descriptions and write the name of the corresponding president on the blank.

Wilson	McKinley	Taylor	T. Roosevelt	Pierce	Garfield
Grant	Jackson	Cleveland	Washington	A. Johnson	Buchanan
Van Buren	Polk	Arthur	Lincoln	B. Harrison	Fillmore

1. _____ This man led the colonial forces during the Revolutionary War. He and the colonial soldiers suffered through the winter of 1777–1778 at Valley Forge while the Red Coats wintered in comfort in Philadelphia. He was the first president of the United States. His wife was Martha, and they lived on the Potomac River at their home known as Mt. Vernon. He is nicknamed "The Father of Our Country."

2. _____ This president was from Tennessee. A general during the War of 1812, he was nicknamed "Old Hickory." Prone to dueling, this president with his hot temper and red hair offended many in Washington when he opened the White House to ordinary citizens at his inauguration.

3. _____ This president from Virginia was president of Princeton University before becoming president of the United States. He was the founder of the League of Nations, but Congress never approved entry into the organization by the United States. He had a stroke while in office, and many thought his wife was carrying out the presidential responsibilities.

4. _____ This president was from the state of New York. He was physically weak as a child, but he became a robust, outdoors man. He gained fame in the Spanish-American War in 1898 when he led a force of American soldiers known as "Rough Riders" up San Juan Hill in Puerto Rico. He was instrumental in establishing the park system in the United States. The building of the Panama Canal was completed while he was in office.

5. _____ This president from Illinois was in office during the Civil War. He delivered the famous Gettysburg Address. This president was assassinated by John Wilkes Booth while watching a play at Ford's Theater. Elected to Congress as a member of the Whig Party, this president was part of a movement to form a new party known as the Republican Party. He was elected president as a member of the Republican Party.

Name_____ Date _____

6. _____Born in Ohio, this president was shot and critically wounded by an assassin in New York on September 6, 1901. He died from the wound on September 14, 1901. The Spanish-American War was fought while this man was president. Hawaii was annexed, and Puerto Rico, the Philippines, and Guam were also acquired by the United States while this man was president.

7. _____This man was elected as the twenty-second president in 1885. He was defeated in 1888 by Benjamin Harrison, who became the twenty-third president. Although he got more popular votes than Harrison, the votes were distributed so that Harrison had more electoral votes. Since Harrison had the most electoral votes, he was declared the winner. In 1893, this man again ran for president and won a second term in office as the twenty-fourth president.

8. _____This man was elected vice president in 1881. Shortly after the election, the president was shot and later died from the gunshot wound. This man then became president, serving from 1881 to 1885. He was nicknamed "Elegant Arthur."

9. _____Born in a log cabin, this man worked very hard to gain a college education. He was a clergyman, a college president, a general in the Union army, and he served in the House of Representatives and Senate. He was shot by a man who was seeking to be appointed to a political office. He did not die immediately from the gunshot. Instead, he lingered until September of 1881. Elected president in 1881, he served only 200 days. His nickname was "Preacher President."

10. _____Known as "Old Kinderhook," this president from New York was elected president in 1837. He was vice president for a popular president known as "Old Hickory." However, "Old Kinderhook" was considered by many to be snobbish when compared to "Old Hickory." Some know this president by the nickname "The Little Magician."

11. _____Born in North Carolina, this president's family moved to Tennessee. Elected as president, he served from 1845 to 1849. This president was in favor of expanding the size of the United States. He felt that Texas and the Oregon Territory should be part of the United States. During his term in office, a war with Mexico was fought and the Rio Grande River became the border between Mexico and the United States.

12. _____Elected president in 1869, this man had been the commanding general of the Union Army in the Civil War. Although he had become famous for his leadership as a general, he was not as successful as president. Extremely loyal to his friends, he often took advice from people who were not as honest as he was. Even though his term in office was marked by many scandals, he was not personally guilty of any act of dishonesty. He was elected for a second term in 1872. He was nicknamed "Uncle Sam."

Name _____ Date _____

13. _____This man became president when Lincoln was assassinated. A poor man with little education, he was first elected as a senator from Tennessee. When Tennessee seceded from the Union, this man did not resign from the Senate. He was nominated as vice president in 1864. He was the first president to be impeached by the House of Representatives. However, the vote in the Senate to remove him from office failed by one vote.

14. _____This president served when North Dakota, South Dakota, Montana, Washington, Idaho, and Wyoming became states. He defeated President Cleveland to win the presidency. He was, in turn, defeated by Cleveland when he ran for a second term.

15. _____This president gained fame as a general in the Mexican-American War. He was nominated by the Whig Party in 1848. Slavery was becoming a major issue in the new territory that was gained when the Mexican War ended.

16. _____A vice president, this man became president when President Taylor died. A major issue of the times was whether California would enter the Union as a free or slave state. A compromise was presented by Senator Clay that brought California into the Union as a free state. When this man became president, he was in favor of the Compromise of 1850.

17. _____The Kansas and Nebraska Act in 1854 caused great conflict over the issue of slavery. The two major political parties of the time were the Whigs and the Democrats. Many Whigs and Democrats in the North insisted that the Kansas and Nebraska territory remain free from slavery. In the South, members of the Whig and Democratic parties wanted the territories open to slavery. The split among the members of each party helped elect this man president. Although this man was a Democrat, the split in the Whig Party resulted in the formation of the Republican Party while he was president.

18. _____Minnesota and Oregon became states while this man was president, and the famous Dred Scott decision was rendered by the Supreme Court while he was in office. Dred Scott was a slave. His owner took him from Missouri, which was a slave state, to live in the free Illinois and Wisconsin territory. Scott later returned to Missouri and claimed he was a free man because he had lived in the Illinois and Wisconsin territory for a number of years. The Supreme Court determined that Scott was not a free man. The abolitionist, John Brown, attacked Harpers Ferry, Virginia, hoping to arm slaves and create a rebellion. Conflicts between those who were anti-slavery and those who were pro-slavery divided the nation during this man's term as president.

Name_____ Date _____

Presidential Time Line

Complete the time line below that shows the terms of office for the presidents of the United States. Place the name of each president in the correct circle. In the box beside each date and name, write things you have found out about the president. One has been completed for you.

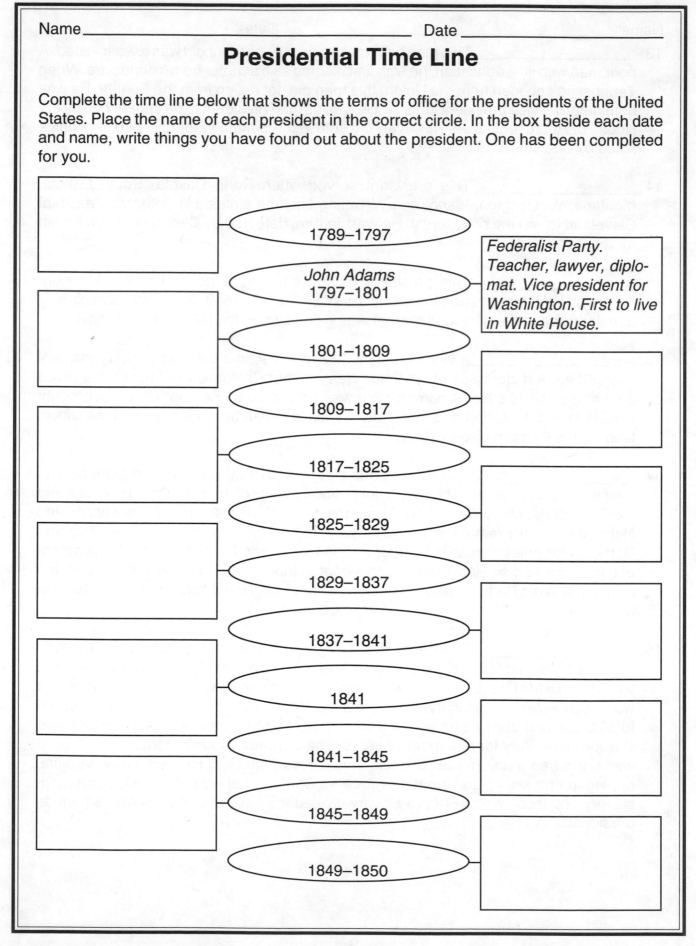

1789–1797

John Adams
1797–1801

Federalist Party. Teacher, lawyer, diplomat. Vice president for Washington. First to live in White House.

1801–1809

1809–1817

1817–1825

1825–1829

1829–1837

1837–1841

1841

1841–1845

1845–1849

1849–1850

Name _____ Date _____

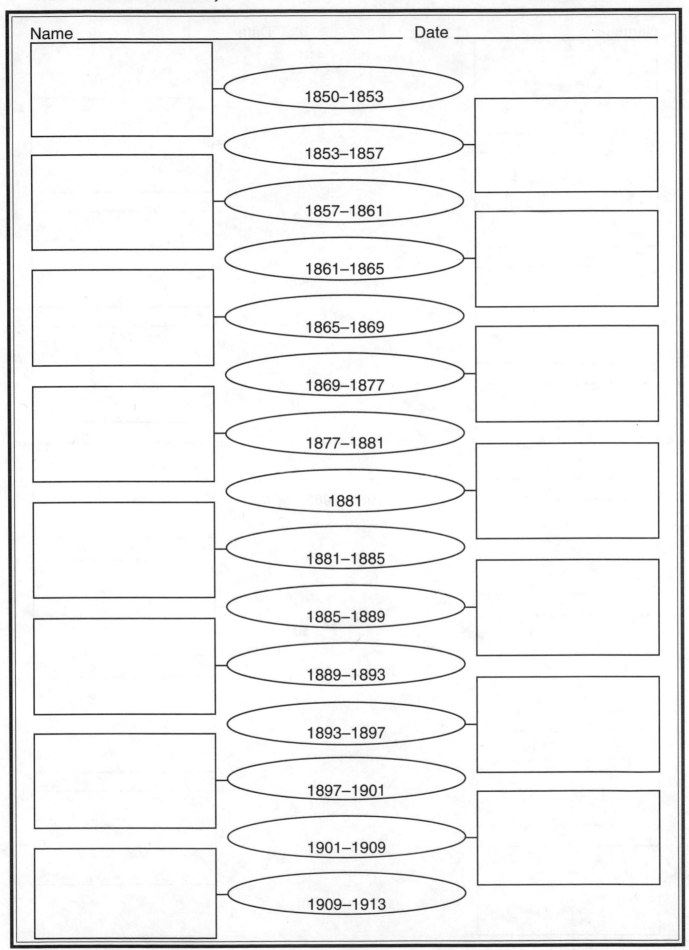

1850–1853

1853–1857

1857–1861

1861–1865

1865–1869

1869–1877

1877–1881

1881

1881–1885

1885–1889

1889–1893

1893–1897

1897–1901

1901–1909

1909–1913

Name _____ Date _____

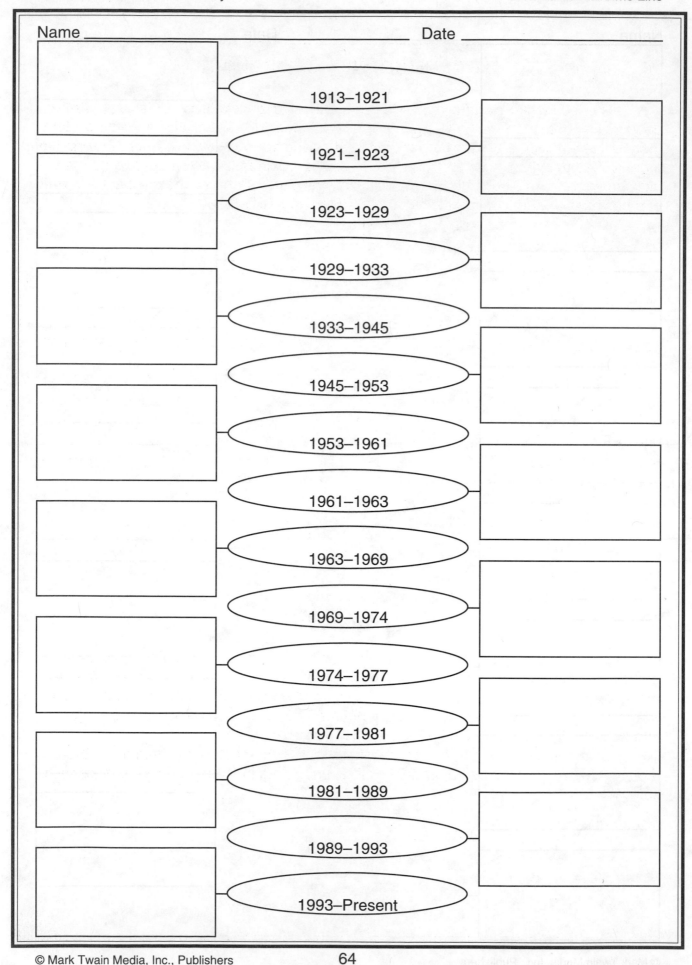

1913–1921

1921–1923

1923–1929

1929–1933

1933–1945

1945–1953

1953–1961

1961–1963

1963–1969

1969–1974

1974–1977

1977–1981

1981–1989

1989–1993

1993–Present

Name_____ Date _____

Understanding Capitalism

The economic system in the United States is **capitalistic**. This is a different economic system than one finds in many other countries. In a capitalistic economic system, there is free enterprise, private property ownership, and freedom of choice. **Free enterprise** means that people have the freedom to start a business. **Private property** means individuals can own a home, farm, or business. **Freedom of choice** means that the owner of a business or farm can decide what to produce and sell.

Match the examples in Column B with the terms in Column A.

Column A	**Column B**
_____ 1. Free enterprise	A. Buying a home
_____ 2. Private property	B. Deciding to start an ice cream parlor
_____ 3. Freedom of choice	C. A farmer chooses to grow corn rather than beans.

In the United States, when individuals make the decision to invest money to begin a new business, they are called **entrepreneurs**. These are individuals who are willing to risk their money to make more money. The individual who invests money to start a business often begins and does most of the work. If the business is successful, the entrepreneur will hire **workers**. For a business to be successful, there must be consumers. **Consumers** are the ones who buy the product the business is producing and/or selling.

Match the examples in Column B with the terms in Column A.

Column A	**Column B**
_____ 4. Consumer	D. Individual who is paid to perform a job
_____ 5. Entrepreneur	E. Individual who buys from a business
_____ 6. Worker	F. Individual who risks money to start a business

In an economy, there must be a **market**. This term refers to the place where sellers and buyers come together. In many cities, there is a large produce market where buyers go to buy vegetables and fruit. When an individual goes to buy a car, the business is a market where the seller and buyer meet. Today buyers and sellers come together through the Internet. The Internet then becomes a market.

Before investing money and time, an entrepreneur must try to determine if there is a market for the product being produced. Will consumers buy the product the business is selling?

65

Name_____ Date _____

Place the letter "B" (buyer), "S" (seller), or "M" (market) on each of the blanks to describe each statement.

_____ 7. Grocery store

_____ 8. Car salesman

_____ 9. Shoe salesman

_____ 10. Man peddling oranges

_____ 11. One who pays for purchases

_____ 12. Individual selecting a watch on the Internet

_____ 13. Farmer delivering wheat to elevator

_____ 14. Internet location where items for sale are priced and described

_____ 15. Restaurant

Terms to Know

monopoly	competition	profit	demand	supply
bankrupt	inflation	recession	depression	expenses

The market system in the United States is based on the idea that sellers compete for buyers. To stay in business, sellers must make a **profit** (money left over after expenses are paid). However, they must have something to sell that buyers want to purchase. In a **monopoly**, there is only one seller of a product, so the consumer must purchase the product from that seller or do without. In a **competitive** system, there are several sellers with similar products, and sellers must think of ways to encourage buyers to purchase their products. Advertising the advantages of a product, selling a product for a lower price, and emphasizing quality are some of the ways sellers encourage buyers.

1. List examples of advertisements found in magazines and newspapers that sellers use to encourage buyers to buy their products.

2. Choose three of the above advertisements that are most likely to encourage you to buy the product. Tell why the advertisement makes you want to buy the product.

   a._____

   _____

   b._____

   _____

   c._____

   _____

Name _____ Date _____

Sellers must make a profit to stay in business. **Profit** is the money left after expenses are paid. **Expenses** include salaries, items purchased to make a product, or the cost of the product that will be resold. Many times competition forces the seller to sell products for less than the cost of producing the product. When this happens, the seller loses money. Then the seller must use savings or borrow money to stay in business. If the seller uses all of the available savings and cannot borrow money, the seller may not be able to pay the expenses and loans. When this happens, the seller goes out of business and may be **bankrupt**.

Sally and Sam own an ice cream parlor. They advertise that all of the ice cream they sell is made at the parlor. Place an "E" (expense) by each item below that would be an expense for the owners.

_____ 3. Milk bought to make the ice cream

_____ 4. Salaries for workers

_____ 5. Soap to clean the ice cream dipper

_____ 6. Paper hats worn by workers

_____ 7. Electricity bill for the shop

_____ 8. Money to pay for taxi fare from home to ice cream parlor

Name_____ Date _____

Capitalism Crossword Puzzle

Use the clues below to complete the crossword puzzle about capitalism. You may need to refer to information on pages 65 to 67 or other resources to find the answers.

ACROSS

1. When there is more than one seller of the same type of product
4. Place where the seller and buyer come together
6. Refers to the amount of a product that buyers are willing to buy at different prices
8. Individual who is paid to perform a job
9. Refers to a situation when a business does not have enough money to pay its bills
12. Refers to what it costs to produce and sell a product
15. A prolonged period of slowing business, widespread unemployment, and falling prices and wages

DOWN

2. When there is only one seller of a product
3. When the amount of money needed to buy the same item continues to increase
5. Individual who risks money to start a business
7. The money left over after all expenses are paid
10. A temporary slow-down in economic activity
11. An economic system in which there is free enterprise, private property ownership, and freedom of choice
13. Refers to the amount of a product that sellers are willing to produce at different prices
14. Individual who buys from a business

Name_____ Date _____

Ownership of Business

Most businesses in the United States are owned by individuals. Some of these business are owned by one person, and some are owned by two or more individuals. When a business is owned by one person, it is called a **sole proprietorship**. When a business is owned by two or more individuals, it is called a **partnership**. In a partnership, there is usually an agreement between partners about the responsibilities of the partners, how profits will be distributed, and what will happen if a partner wants out of the business.

Sole Proprietorship

Sally decided to start an ice cream business. She quit her job and, with her savings and a loan from the bank, bought equipment and supplies and rented a building in the mall where there would be a market for the ice cream. Sally managed the business and also waited on customers. Each day she spent long hours, and the business began to grow. After two years, Sally was able to hire two helpers who served the customers. The business became successful, and after 10 years, Sally wanted someone to share the operation of the business with, so she decided to find someone who would become a partner with her in the business.

Partnership

Sally and Sam have owned their ice cream parlor as partners for five years. When they started the business, they agreed to share equally all expenses, profits, and the work needed to keep the business going.

The business has grown, and Sally has saved enough money to retire and travel. Sam is younger and wants to continue working. However, he does not have enough money to buy Sally's part of the business. Sally is willing to remain as part owner of the business. Since she will be retired and traveling, she will not be able to work in the business. Sally and Sam decide that they must develop a new agreement on how the partnership will work.

1. Work with a partner and each of you assume the role of either Sally or Sam. Suggest some possible new ways the agreement could be written so that both could continue as owners. Take into consideration how expenses, profits, and responsibilities would be divided if Sam continues operating the business and Sally retires and travels.

_____

_____

_____

_____

_____

Name_____ Date _____

Corporations

Many large companies in the United States are **corporations**. A corporation is much different than a business that an individual owns or a business that is a partnership. Corporations have **stockholders** who own shares of **stock** in the business. However, the stockholders as owners do not run the business. The stockholders in a corporation elect a **board of directors** who are also stockholders in the corporation. The board of directors then hire people to run the business. Holders of **preferred stock** are paid a guaranteed dividend before the remaining profits are distributed among the common stock holders. **Common stocks** do not guarantee a dividend will be paid, but owners of common stock do have voting privileges.

Sally and Sam Form a Corporation

Sally and Sam's new partnership worked very well. In fact, their ice cream business became so successful, they now own ice cream parlors in 12 large cities. In fact, the ice cream parlors all have the same name "S and S Homemade Ice Cream." Sally is still retired and traveling, but now Sam must travel to the 12 cities, meeting with the managers hired to run each of the ice cream parlors.

Sam now wants to retire, so he and Sally decide they will change their business from a partnership to a corporation. They must get approval from the states where they have ice cream parlors to form a corporation. They must determine the number of stocks that will be sold. They must also determine how the board of directors will be elected. Once the stock is sold, Sally and Sam will be two of the many owners of the corporation.

Sam and Sally decided to sell 100,000 shares of stock in the corporation. They decided that each share will sell for $20. When voting for members of the board of directors, each share will be one vote. They decide that they do not want to lose control of the corporation, so each buys 25,001 shares. The two of them have 50,002 shares to cast as votes for the board of directors. Since Sally wants to remain retired and continue to travel, she can cast her shares as votes for Sam. If Sam casts the shares he owns as votes for himself, he will be elected to the board of directors.

Match the definitions in Column B with the terms in Column A.

Column A
_____ 2. Partnership
_____ 3. Corporation
_____ 4. Stockholders
_____ 5. Board of Directors
_____ 6. Stock
_____ 7. Common Stock
_____ 8. Preferred Stock

Column B
A. Stock with guaranteed dividends
B. Stock with voting privileges, but no guaranteed dividends
C. A certificate indicating the owner is a part owner of a corporation
D. Members elected by the owners of a corporation
E. When two or more persons own a business
F. Those who own stock in a corporation
G. Business owned by stockholders

Name_____ Date _____

Learning About the Stock Market

Many corporations are listed on the **stock market**. Stock in companies is bought and sold on one of the **stock exchanges**. Stock exchanges provide the market for stocks. Most large cities, like New York and Chicago, have stock exchanges.

The following are examples of five companies with stock that was bought and sold on one of the stock exchanges. The information that appears was taken from a newspaper with a section that lists the stocks that can be bought or sold on the stock exchange. It is important to learn how to read the stocks as they appear in the newspaper. The following are terms you must know in order to read a stock quotation.

| | stock name | dividend | yield | | sales | |
| | high | low | close | | net change | |

Stock	Dividend	Yield %	Sales	High	Low	Close	Net Change
A	1.48	7.6	190,000	19 13/16	19 7/16	19 7/16	1/8
B	1.74	6.5	328,000	27 1/4	26 7/8	26 15/16	5/16
C	0.96	5.7	39,000	17	16 5/8	16 13/16	1/16
D	0.80	1.1	416,000	75 5/8	70 5/8	74 3/8	-1 1/4
E	0.52	1.4	482,000	39 3/8	37 1/2	37 1/2	-1 7/8

1. List the names of the "companies" with stock listed in this example.

_____

2. The stock with the highest closing price is _____ .

3. The stock with the greatest net change in price is _____ .

4. The stock paying the greatest dividend is_____ .

5. The stock with the greatest number of sales is _____ .

6. The high for "A" stock was _____ , and the low was _____ .

7. The high for "B" stock was _____ , and the low was _____ .

8. The high for "C" stock was _____ , and the low was _____ .

9. The high for "D" stock was _____ , and the low was _____ .

10. The high for "E" stock was _____ , and the low was _____ .

Name_____ Date _____

Determining Stock Prices from Quotes

Stock prices are quoted (listed) using fractions (1/2, 15/16, etc.). To convert the price of a stock to dollars and cents, it is necessary to change the fraction to a decimal.

Example: The closing selling price for a stock is quoted as 10 3/4. The fraction 3/4 must be changed to cents. First change 3/4 to a decimal by dividing 3 by 4.

$$\begin{array}{r} 0.75 \\ 4\overline{)3.00} \\ \underline{28} \\ 20 \\ \underline{20} \\ 0 \end{array}$$

So in dollars and cents, 10 3/4 is $10.75.

Complete the following. Change the quote to decimals or dollars and cents. Change dollars and cents to quotes.

1. 1/2 = _____   2. 1/4 = _____   3. 3/8 = _____

4. 5/8 = _____   5. 7/8 = _____   6. 7 1/2 = $ _____

7. 12 1/4 = $ _____   8. 43 3/8 = $ _____   9. 64 7/8 = $ _____

10. $23.50 = _____   11. $56.25 = _____   12. $9.40 = _____

Refer to the stock quotations below and answer the questions that follow.

Stock	Dividend	Yield %	Sales	High	Low	Close	Net Change
F	2.10	6.7	79,000	31 5/8	30 7/8	31 3/16	-7/16
G	5.30	5.6	168,000	96 1/2	90 5/16	93 15/16	-2 9/16
H	0.79	1.4	43,000	58 1/2	57 1/4	58 5/16	-3/16
I	0.65	4.0	310,000	16 3/8	16 1/4	16 1/4	-1/8
J	1.03	4.0	95,000	26 1/16	25 1/2	25 15/16	7/16
K	3.00	7.3	124,000	41 1/4	40 9/16	41 1/8	9/16
L	0.55	0.7	81,000	83 1/8	82 5/16	83	11/16
M	2.25	1.7	153,000	61 1/8	59	60 1/2	2 1/16

13. "F" stock lost _____ cents in value on this trading day.

14. "G" stock lost $ _____ in value on this trading day.

15. The closing value for stock "H" on this trading day was $ _____.

16. The lowest value for stock "I" on this trading day was $ _____.

17. The highest value for stock "J" on this trading day was $ _____.

18. The closing value for stock "K" on this trading day was $ _____.

19. "L" stock gained _____ cents in value on this trading day.

20. "M" stock gained $ _____ in value on this trading day.

Name _____ Date _____

Stock Growth, Dividends, and Yield

When buying stock, many investors are interested in the **dividend** the stock will pay. Others are interested in the **yield**. Some are more interested in the possibility of **growth in value**. Interest in each of these depends on the individual investor.

Dividends

The **dividend** is the amount of money that an owner of stock receives when the company makes money. The amount of the dividend will vary from year to year. The board of directors determines the dividend that will be paid to stockholders.

Example: A share of stock is priced at $50.00. The board of directors determine that for a given year the dividend paid will be $4.00 per share. Next year the board will again determine the amount of the dividend that will be paid.

Assume that you own the five shares of stock listed in the table below. You have owned the stock for three years. Each year you have received a dividend check for the amount listed. Determine the average dividend you have received for each of the shares of stock.

Price of Stock Per Share	Dividends Paid			Three-Year Dividend Average
1. $14.00	$1.00	$0.75	$0.55	_____
2. $40.00	$2.50	$1.25	$0.75	_____
3. $22.00	$1.50	$1.00	$0.80	_____
4. $88.00	$4.00	$2.50	$3.00	_____
5. $212.00	$8.00	$6.00	$7.00	_____

Name_____ Date _____

Yield

Yield is a figure that compares the dividend earned to the price of the stock. To find yield, divide the current annual dividend by the price of the stock, and then multiply by 100 to get a percentage.

Example: A share of stock is priced at $50.00. The dividend is $4.00.

$$4 \div 50 = 0.08 \times 100 = 8\% \text{ yield}$$

Refer to the table below and determine the yield for the last year for each of the five stocks you own.

Price of Stock Per Share	Dividends Paid			Yearly Yield
1. $14.00	$1.00	$0.75	$0.55	_____
2. $40.00	$2.50	$1.25	$0.75	_____
3. $22.00	$1.50	$1.00	$0.80	_____
4. $88.00	$4.00	$2.50	$3.00	_____
5. $212.00	$8.00	$6.00	$7.00	_____

Growth in Value

Growth in value of a share of stock is important to investors who are going to keep the stock for a long period of time. These individuals may own the stock for many years, so they hope to see it increase in value.

Assume you own the following five shares of stock. You want stock that will grow in value over a period of years. The price per share for a three-year period is shown in the chart below. Place a + or - on the blank to indicate if the share of stock is increasing or decreasing in value.

Price of Stock Per Share			Dividends Paid			Growth of Stock
1. $14.00	$18.00	$19.00	$1.00	$0.75	$0.55	_____
2. $40.00	$38.00	$23.00	$2.50	$1.25	$0.75	_____
3. $22.00	$30.00	$32.00	$1.50	$1.00	$0.80	_____
4. $88.00	$77.00	$78.00	$4.00	$2.50	$3.00	_____
5. $212.00	$198.00	$178.00	$8.00	$6.00	$7.00	_____

74

Name_____ Date_____

Reading Quotes From the Stock Market

1. Listed below are four large U.S. corporations. Find the stock market section in a newspaper. For a given day, list the price paid per share for stock in each of the companies listed. Determine the closing price in dollars and cents for each share.

Corporation	Share Price/Fraction	Dollars/Cents Per Share
a) Ford Motor	_____	$ _____
b) Chrysler	_____	$ _____
c) McDonnell Douglas	_____	$ _____
d) Shell Oil	_____	$ _____

2. Find a newspaper and turn to the section that shows the companies that have stock that is bought and sold on the stock market. List 10 of the companies and complete the blanks in the chart below.

Corporation	Share Price/Fraction	Dollars/Cents Per Share
a) _____	_____	_____
b) _____	_____	_____
c) _____	_____	_____
d) _____	_____	_____
e) _____	_____	_____
f) _____	_____	_____
g) _____	_____	_____
h) _____	_____	_____
i) _____	_____	_____
j) _____	_____	_____

Name_____ Date _____

Stock Market Crossword Puzzle

Use the clues below to complete the crossword puzzle about the stock market. You may need to refer to pages 71 to 75 to find the answers.

ACROSS

2. Owners of this stock receive a fixed dividend (two words).
7. A figure that compares the dividend earned to the price of the stock
8. Where stocks are bought and sold (two words)
10. Owners of this stock are not guaranteed a fixed dividend (two words).

DOWN

1. Interest paid on stock owned is called a _____.
3. This word refers to the chance one takes when buying stock.
4. Indicates ownership in a corporation
5. Growth in _____ is important to investors who are going to keep the stock for a long period of time.
6. The change in value of stock from one day to the next is called _____ _____.
8. Owners of a corporation
9. The owners of this type of business own shares of stock and elect a board of directors to run the business.
10. Column in a stock quote that refers to the price of a share of stock at the end of the day's market

Name_____ Date _____

Learning About Supply and Demand

When running a business, it is important to know about supply and demand. The term **demand** means the amount of a good or service people are willing to buy at a certain price. **Supply** is the amount of goods or services that will be produced to be sold at a certain price.

Write the term supply or demand on each of the blanks according to what is being discussed in each statement.

_____ 1. One thousand Great Taste candy bars will be bought when the price is $0.50 each.

_____ 2. Two thousand Great Taste candy bars will be produced when the buyers are willing to pay $0.75 for each bar.

_____ 3. Five hundred Great Taste candy bars will be bought when the price is $0.65 each.

_____ 4. Five thousand Great Taste candy bars will be produced when buyers are willing to pay $1.00 for each bar.

_____ 5. Two hundred fifty Great Taste candy bars will be bought when the price is $0.80 each.

_____ 6. Five thousand pairs of Fast Jog running shoes will be bought when the price is $95.00 per pair.

_____ 7. Ten thousand pairs of Fast Jog running shoes will be produced when buyers are willing to pay $110.00 for each pair.

_____ 8. Eight hundred athletic shirts are available for sale in a store.

_____ 9. Two hundred athletic shirts were sold last week.

_____ 10. Two stores stock the same athletic shirt. One store has 500 shirts for sale, and the other store has 250 shirts.

Name_____ Date _____

Great Taste Candies

Rosita Garcia owns Great Taste Candies. Rosita has owned her shop for 15 years and has built a thriving business. She makes her own candy using a special recipe. Her customers include people living in the neighborhood as well as people who drive in from outside the neighborhood to buy her famous candy.

Rosita sells candy in one-pound boxes. She has been making and selling 1,000 boxes of candy at a price of $2.00 per pound. She has been averaging sales of $2,000 per month. After paying all expenses, her net income has been $800 per month.

The $800 per month profit allows Rosita to pay her bills, own a small comfortable home, a small automobile, and have some money for bowling and eating out one time per week. She cannot increase the number of boxes of candy she sells at a price of $2.00 per box. Rosita could sell 1,500 boxes of candy each month if she would lower the price to $1.25. However, she would have to work many more hours to make the extra candy. Working the extra hours would mean that she would not have as much time to bowl, eat out, and enjoy her other interests.

Circle the correct response in the following statements.

1. If Rosita decided to produce 1,500 boxes of candy and keep the price at $2.00 per box, she would increase the (supply/demand).

2. If Rosita is going to increase demand for her candy, she must (increase/decrease) the price.

The chart below shows the number of boxes of candy that Rosita can sell at different prices.

Price Per Box	Number of Boxes Bought
$4.00	100
$3.50	200
$3.00	270
$2.50	750
$2.00	1000
$1.50	1250
$1.25	1500

3. The above chart shows that, as the price decreases, the (supply/demand) for candy increases.

Name_____ Date _____

The chart below shows the number of boxes of candy that Rosita is willing to supply at different prices.

Price Per Box	Number of Boxes Supplied
$1.25	100
$1.50	200
$2.00	1000
$2.50	1100
$3.00	1200
$3.50	1250
$4.00	1500

4. Plot the above data on the graph below. The first one has been completed for you. After you have plotted all the points, connect the points with a line.

Graph I: **Supply of Great Taste Candy at Various Prices**

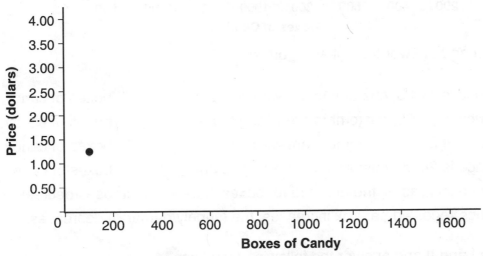

Refer to Graph I and answer the following questions.

5. When the price is $1.25, Rosita is willing to supply _____ boxes of candy.

6. When the price is $2.00, Rosita is willing to supply _____ boxes of candy.

7. When the price is $3.00, Rosita is willing to supply _____ boxes of candy.

8. When the price is $4.00, Rosita is willing to supply _____ boxes of candy.

9. When the price increases, Rosita is willing to (supply/demand) more boxes of candy.

10. When the price received per box increases, the (supply/demand) increases.

Name _____ Date _____

11. Use the data in the demand chart on page 78 to complete the graph below. The first one has been completed for you. After you have plotted all the points, connect the points with a line.

Graph II: **Demand for Great Taste Candy at Various Prices**

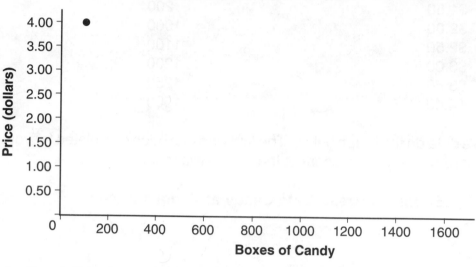

Refer to Graph II and answer the following questions.

12. When the price is $1.25, customers are willing to buy _____ boxes of candy.

13. When the price is $2.00, customers are willing to buy _____ boxes of candy.

14. When the price is $3.00, customers are willing to buy _____ boxes of candy.

15. When the price is $4.00, customers are willing to buy _____ boxes of candy.

16. When the price increases, the demand for boxes of candy (increases/decreases).

17. When the price received per box increases, the (supply/demand) decreases.

Refer to Graphs I and II and answer the following questions.

18. The line in Graph I shows the change in (supply/demand).

19. The line in Graph II shows the changes in (supply/demand).

Locate the point where the line in Graph I crosses the line in Graph II.

20. The number of boxes of candy supplied at the point where the lines cross is _____ boxes.

21. The point where the lines cross shows that customers are willing to pay $ _____ per box when this number of boxes is supplied.

Name_____ Date _____

The last two months, Rosita has continued to sell her candy for $2.00 a box and has continued making 1,000 boxes a month. Her average sales were $1500 per month. However, her expenses have not changed. She has 500 boxes of candy that she has not sold. She is afraid this candy will spoil, and she is considering lowering the price to sell the candy.

22. Has demand or supply changed for Rosita's candy? _____

23. By dropping the price, Rosita hopes to increase (supply/demand).

Rosita decides to lower the price on the 500 boxes by 25 percent per box.

24. The selling price for the 500 boxes of candy will be   a) $1.00   b) $1.75
    c) $1.50   d) $1.25.

Rosita is successful in selling the 500 boxes of candy.

25. By dropping the price, Rosita increased (supply/demand).

26. By dropping the price, Rosita (increased/decreased) profit.

Name_____ Date _____

Learning About Social Security

In the United States, most workers and employers pay Social Security tax that will be used for workers' retirement. This money is taken out of a worker's check and is sent to the federal government. The federal government then places the money in the Social Security fund, which is used to pay retirement benefits when workers retire.

The following chart shows the age at which a worker can retire and receive full Social Security retirement benefits.

Year of Birth	Full Retirement Age
1937	65 years
1938	65 years, 2 months
1939	65 years, 4 months
1940	65 years, 6 months
1941	65 years, 8 months
1942	65 years, 10 months
1943–1954	66 years
1955	66 years, 2 months
1956	66 years, 4 months
1957	66 years, 6 months
1958	66 years, 8 months
1959	66 years, 10 months
1960 and later	67 years

1. Plot the above data on a line graph in the space below and answer the questions that follow. Be sure to connect the plotted points with a line.

Name_____ Date _____

2. The age at which one can retire and receive Social Security is (increasing/decreasing).

3. In what year will you be 67 years of age? _____

4. Assume that the retirement age for the above chart is extended to 1975 and increases two months each year from 1960 to 1975. Create a line graph in the space below to show the change in retirement age from 1960 to 1975.

5. Refer to the graph above and determine the retirement age for individuals born in the years listed below.

Year of Birth	Retirement Age
a) 1961	_____
b) 1964	_____
c) 1967	_____
d) 1969	_____
e) 1970	_____
f) 1973	_____
g) 1975	_____

Name_____ Date _____

How Far Will the Money Go?

Assume the average monthly Social Security retirement check today is $1,000. Assume that the amount of the retirement check is increased three percent per year. Assume that you will retire 50 years from now. You can expect to receive a monthly check of $4,383. Assume that the rate of inflation is also three percent. A candy bar that costs $0.75 today will cost approximately $3.30 50 years from now. The candy bar will cost approximately 4.4 times more in 50 years than it does today.

Complete the chart below for each item. Increase the Cost Today price by 4.4 times to complete the blanks under Cost 50 Years From Now.

Item	Cost Today	Cost 50 Years From Now
1. Candy Bar	$0.75	$3.30
2. Soda	$0.50	_____
3. Jogging Shoes	$75.00	_____
4. Jeans	$35.00	_____
5. Gallon of Gas	$1.10	_____
6. Loaf of Bread	$1.50	_____
7. Television	$500.00	_____
8. Car	$20,000.00	_____
9. Refrigerator	$950.00	_____
10. Dinner at Restaurant	$15.00	_____

You can see from the above chart that, when you retire, things you buy will cost much more. Even though the Social Security check you receive will be larger than it is today, you will likely need more money to live. Most workers find that the Social Security retirement benefit does not make it possible for them to have enough money to enjoy the things they want to do when they retire. Therefore, many workers plan to save money while working so they will have more money when they retire.

Answer Keys

United States Geography (pages 1–2)

1–2. Teacher check

3a. 4
 b. 9
 c. 8
 d. 10
 e. 2
 f. 3
 g. 6
 h. 1
 i. 5
 j. 7

4a. Los Angeles 8,800,000 CA
 b. New York 8,600,000 NY
 c. Chicago 6,300,000 IL
 d. Philadelphia 5,000,000 PA
 e. Detroit 4,400,000 MI
 f. Washington, D.C. 3,850,000 DC
 g. Boston 3,800,000 MA
 h. Houston 3,200,000 TX
 i. Atlanta 2,800,000 GA
 j. Dallas 2,500,000 TX

5. Utah, Montana, New Mexico

6. State may be listed in any order.

a. Idaho: Snake River

b. Kansas: Missouri River

c. California: Colorado River, Pacific Ocean

d. Arizona: Colorado River

e. Oklahoma: Red River

f. Minnesota: Mississippi River, Red River, St. Croix River, Lake Superior, Lake of the Woods

g. Texas: Rio Grande River, Red River, Sabine River, Gulf of Mexico

h. Massachusetts: Atlantic Ocean

United States Crossword Puzzle (page 4)

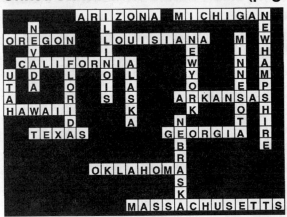

Physical Features in the United States (page 5)

Teacher check map

1. Colorado, Montana
2. Virginia, Tennessee
3. California
4. Nevada
5. California
6. Arkansas, Missouri
7. Florida
8. Utah
9. Minnesota, Michigan
10. Michigan, Illinois, Indiana
11. Ohio, New York
12. New York
13. Michigan
14. Arkansas, Mississippi, Missouri, Iowa
15. Illinois, Ohio, Indiana, Kentucky
16. Nebraska, Iowa, South Dakota
17. Texas, New Mexico
18. New York
19. Colorado, Utah, Arizona, California
20. Washington, Oregon
21. Tennessee, Kentucky
22. Virginia, Maryland
23. Texas, Mississippi, Alabama, Florida
24. California
25. New York, Vermont
26. Louisiana
27. Alaska
28. Washington
29. Hawaii
30. Colorado

U.S. Physical Features Crossword Puzzle (page 6)

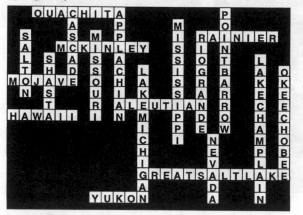

Rivers in the United States (page 7)

1–3. Teacher check map

4. The Rocky Mountains serve as a Continental Divide because they are at a very high elevation. Rivers west of the divide flow from the higher elevation to the lower elevation of the Pacific Ocean. Rivers east of the divide flow from the higher elevation toward the lower elevation of the Mississippi River and the Gulf of Mexico.

Capital Cities (page 8)

1. Des Moines
2. Santa Fe
3. Augusta
4. Sacramento
5. Columbia
6. Concord
7. Pierre
8. Lansing
9. Jefferson City
10. Topeka
11. Phoenix
12. Boise
13. Atlanta
14. Montgomery
15. Montpelier
16. Lincoln
17. Olympia
18. Richmond
19. Providence
20. Frankfort
21. Cheyenne
22. Carson City
23. Baton Rouge
24. Helena
25. Charleston

Head for the Border (page 9)

1. TX, LA, MS, AL, FL
2. ME, NH, MA, RI, CT, NY, NJ, DE, MD, VA, NC, SC, GA, FL
3. AK, HA, WA, OR, CA
4. CA, AZ, NM, TX
5. AK, WA, ID, MT, ND, MN, MI, OH, PA, NY, VT, NH, ME

Regions of the United States (pages 10–12)

1. ME, NH, VT, MA, RI, CT, NY, NJ, PA, DE, MD, WV, VA
2. OH, KY, MI, IN, IL, WI, MN, IA, MO, ND, SD, NE, KS
3. NC, SC, GA, FL, TN, AL, MS, AR, LA
4. WA, ID, MT, OR, WY, CA, NV, UT, CO, AZ, NM, TX, OK

Name That State: Part I (pages 13–14)

1. Kentucky, (a) Frankfort
2. Ohio
3. Virginia, (a) Richmond, (b-f) Any five: Washington, Jefferson, Madison, Monroe, W.H. Harrison, Taylor, Wilson
4. Tennessee, (a) Nashville, (b-d) Jackson, Polk, A. Johnson
5. West Virginia
6–8. Teacher check map

Name That State: Part II (pages 15–16)

1. New Hampshire, (a) Concord
2. Vermont, (a) the Connecticut River, (b) Lake Champlain, (c) Canada
3. Maine, (a) Atlantic, (b-c) Quebec, New Brunswick
4–6. Teacher check maps

Name That State: Part III (pages 17–18)
1. Minnesota, (a) St. Paul
2. Iowa, (a) Des Moines, (b) Mississippi, (c) Missouri
3. Missouri, (a) Jefferson City, (b) St. Louis
4–6. Teacher check map

Name That State: Part IV (pages 19–20)
1. Oregon, (a) Salem, (b) Idaho
2. Washington, (a) Olympia, (b) Columbia
3. Idaho, (a) Boise, (b) Snake
4–6. Teacher check map

Name That State: Part V (pages 21–22)
1. New Jersey, (a) Trenton, (b) Pennsylvania
2. Pennsylvania, (a) Harrisburg, (b) Pittsburgh, (c) Delaware, (d) Philadelphia
3. Delaware
4. Connecticut, (a) Hartford, (b) Connecticut
5–7. Teacher check map

Name That State: Part VI (page 23)
1. Hawaii
2. Alaska
3–5. Teacher check map

Name That State: Part VII (pages 24–25)
1. Arizona
2. California
3. Utah
4. Nevada
5–7. Teacher check maps

Reading and Using Road Maps: Part I (page 26)
1. PA, OH, IN, IL, MO, KS, CO, UT, NV, CA
2. Teacher check map
3. FL, AL, MS, LA, TX, NM, CO, WY, MT, ID, WA
4. Teacher check map

Reading and Using Road Maps: Part II (page 27)
Answers may vary since students may choose alternate highways. Numbers in bold indicate Interstate Highways. Other numbers are U.S. Highways.
1. Highways: **70**, **29**, **90**, 281, 14, 83, 2, 87, **15**, **90**, 93, 12, **84**
States: MO, IA, SD, ND, MT, ID, OR, WA
2. Highways: **35**, 56, 50, **25**, 84, 64, 666, 191, **70**, **15**
States: MO, KS, CO, NM, CO, UT, AZ, NV, CA

Map Measurements (page 28)
1. 200
2. 425
3. d
4. 100
5. d
6. 350
7. a
8. 1,250
9. 1.6
10. 16
11. 160
12. 1,600
13. 560
14. 320
15. 680
16. 2,000

Size of the United States Compared to Other Nations (page 29)
1a. 10
 b. 1
 c. 6
 d. 4
 e. 8
 f. 3
 g. 5
 h. 2
 i. 7
 j. 9
2. 3
3. 3,418,000,000

Using Graphs to Show Information: Circle Graphs (page 31)

Numbers are rounded off, so the totals may not be exactly 100% or 360°.

1a. 2.6%   9.36°
 b. 35.9%   129.24°
 c. 4.3%   15.48°
 d. 5.8%   20.88°
 e. 3.66%   13.176°
 f. 7.7%   27.72°
 g. 4.7%   16.92°
 h. 27.6%   99.36°
 i. 4.2%   15.12°
 j. 3.45%   12.42°

2–6. Teacher check graphs

Learning About Population Pyramids (page 32)

1. b
2. a
3. b
4. No
5. Yes
6. Yes
7. No

Line Graphs and Population (pages 33–36)

Teacher check graphs and maps.

4. Column II

Texas	22,620,000
California	39,440,000
Arizona	5,220,000
New Mexico	2,088,000
Nevada	1,972,000
Utah	2,436,000

7. Column II

Florida	16,385,000
Alabama	4,972,000
Colorado	4,633,000
Idaho	1,356,000
Oregon	3,729,000

9. b

Population Density (pages 37–38)

1a. 1,000 b. 1,000 people per square mile.
2a. 2,500   b. 2,500
3. 625
4a. 73   b. 39   c. 15
 d. 15   e. 25
5. Texas
6. New Mexico, Nevada

7a. 249   7
 b. 331   5
 c. 22   10
 d. 271   6
 e. 856   2
 f. 73   8
 g. 49   9
 h. 743   3
 i. 469   4
 j. 2,107   1
8. Bangladesh
9. Russia

Elevation and Contour Maps (pages 39–41)

1–4. Teacher check diagram
5. a
6. a
7–9. Teacher check diagram
10. #
11. The contour lines are closer together at the # location, which means the terrain is steeper.
12–22. Teacher check diagram

More Elevation Practice (page 42)

1. Teacher check diagram

Understanding Temperature Maps (pages 43–44)

Teacher check maps and cities indicated

The Government of the United States Legislative Branch (page 45)

1. b
2. c
3. a

The House of Representatives (pages 45–46)

4. b
5. c
6. a
7. a
8. b
9. a
10. b

11–12. Answers will vary. Teacher check

13a. California, b. It has the largest population.

c. Wyoming, d. It has the smallest population.

House of Representatives Review (page 47)

1. legislative
2. vested
3. Congress
4. chosen
5. attained
6. twenty-five
7. seven
8. citizen
9. inhabitant
10. No. He has not been a citizen for seven years, and he is not an inhabitant of Vermont.
11. Yes. She is old enough, lives in the state, and has been a citizen long enough.
12. Yes. He will have been a citizen for seven years by the time of the election.

The Senate (page 48)

1. two
2. six
3. one
4. thirty
5. nine
6. president
7. tie
8. impeachments
9. Chief Justice
10. Senate

Legislation (page 49)

1. House of Representatives
2. Senate
3. House of Representatives
4. Senate
5. House of Representatives
6. Senate
7. president

8. president
9. D
10. F
11. I
12. A
13. B
14. G
15. H
16. E
17. C

Executive Branch (pages 50–51)

1. executive
2. four
3. 35
4. electors
5. Electoral College
6. representatives, senators
7. No. He is not old enough.
8. No. He is not a natural-born citizen.
9. Yes
10. Representative
11. President, Senator, Representative
12. President, Senator, Representative
13. None

Branches of the U.S. Government Crossword Puzzle (page 52)

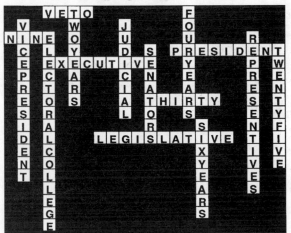

Electing the President and Vice President: Electoral College Votes (pages 54–58)

1. California, New York, Texas, Florida, Pennsylvania

2. 167
3. 270
4a. California   54
  b. New York   33
  c. Texas   32
  d. Florida   25
  e. Pennsylvania   23
  f. Illinois   22
  g. Ohio   21
  h. Michigan   18
  i. New Jersey   15
  j. North Carolina   14
5a. California   34,000,000
  b. Texas   19,500,000
  c. New York   18,800,000
  d. Florida   14,500,000
  e. Pennsylvania   12,100,000
  f. Illinois   11,900,000
  g. Ohio   11,500,000
  h. Michigan   9,800,000
  i. New Jersey   8,100,000
  j. Georgia   7,500,000
6–7. Teacher check graphs
8a. Alaska   3
  b. Delaware   3
  c. District of Columbia   3
  d. Montana   3
  e. North Dakota   3
  f. South Dakota   3
  g. Vermont   3
  h. Wyoming   3
9a. Wyoming   480,000
  b. District of Columbia   530,000
  c. Vermont   585,000
  d. North Dakota   600,000
  e. Alaska   615,000
  f. South Dakota   735,000
  g. Delaware   740,000
  h. Montana   880,000
10. Teacher check graph
11. F
12. T
13. T
14. T
15. F

16. increase; as population increases, the number of representatives in a state increases, and the number of electoral votes will also increase.

U.S. Presidents (pages 59–61)
1. Washington
2. Jackson
3. Wilson
4. T. Roosevelt
5. Lincoln
6. McKinley
7. Cleveland
8. Arthur
9. Garfield
10. Van Buren
11. Polk
12. Grant
13. A. Johnson
14. B. Harrison
15. Taylor
16. Fillmore
17. Pierce
18. Buchanan

Presidential Time Line (pages 62–64)
Teacher check time line and facts listed.

Understanding Capitalism (pages 65–66)
1. B
2. A
3. C
4. E
5. F
6. D
7. M
8. S
9. S
10. S
11. B
12. B
13. S
14. M
15. M

Terms to Know (pages 66–67)
1–2. Teacher check
3–8. All are expenses.

Capitalism Crossword Puzzle (page 68)

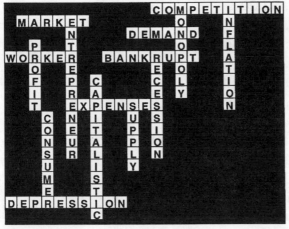

Ownership of Business (pages 69–70)
1. Teacher check
2. E
3. G
4. F
5. D
6. C
7. B
8. A

Learning About the Stock Market (page 71)
1. A, B, C, D, E
2. D
3. E
4. B
5. E
6. 19 13/16, 19 7/16
7. 27 1/4, 26 7/8
8. 17, 16 5/8
9. 75 5/8, 70 5/8
10. 39 3/8, 37 1/2

Determining Stock Prices From Quotes (page 72)
1. 0.50 or $0.50
2. 0.25 or $0.25
3. 0.375 or $0.38
4. 0.625 or $0.63
5. 0.875 or $0.88
6. $7.50
7. $12.25
8. $43.38
9. $64.88
10. 23 1/2
11. 56 1/4
12. 9 4/10 or 9 2/5
13. 44
14. 2.56
15. 58.31
16. 16.25
17. 26.06
18. 41.13
19. 69
20. 2.06

Stock Growth, Dividends, and Yield Dividends (page 73)
1. $0.77
2. $1.50
3. $1.10
4. $3.17
5. $7.00

Yield (page 74)
1. 3.9%
2. 1.9%
3. 3.6%
4. 3.4%
5. 3.3%

Growth in Value (page 74)
1. +
2. -
3. +
4. - then +
5. -

Reading Quotes From the Stock Market (page 75)
1–2. Answers will vary. Teacher check

Stock Market Crossword Puzzle (page 76)

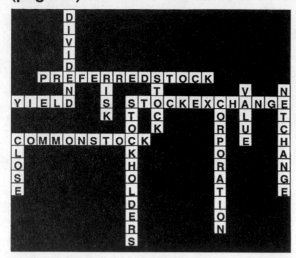

Learning About Supply and Demand (page 77)

1. demand
2. supply
3. demand
4. supply
5. demand
6. demand
7. supply
8. supply
9. demand
10. supply

Greate Taste Candies (pages 78–81)

1. supply
2. decrease
3. demand
4. Teacher check graph
5. 100
6. 1,000
7. 1,200
8. 1,500
9. supply
10. supply
11. Teacher check graph
12. 1,500
13. 1,000 ·
14. 270
15. 100

16. decreases
17. demand
18. supply
19. demand
20. 1,000
21. $2.00
22. demand
23. demand
24. c
25. demand
26. decreased

Learning About Social Security (pages 82–83)

1. Teacher check graph
2. increasing
3. Answers will vary.
4. Teacher check graph
5a. 67 years, 2 months
  b. 67 years, 8 months
  c. 68 years, 2 months
  d. 68 years, 6 months
  e. 68 years, 8 months
  f. 69 years, 2 months
  g. 69 years, 6 months

How Far Will the Money Go? (page 84)

2. $2.20
3. $330.00
4. $154.00
5. $4.84
6. $6.60
7. $2,200.00
8. $88,000.00
9. $4,180.00
10. $66.00